KATHERINE MANSFIELD

Andrew Bennett

Northcote House
in association with the
British Council

© Copyright 2004 by Andrew Bennett

First published in 2004 by Northcote House Publishers Ltd, Horndon, Tavistock, Devon, PL19 9NQ, United Kingdom.
Tel: +44 (0) 1822 810066 Fax: +44 (0) 1822 810034.

British Library Cataloguing-in-Publication Data
A catalogue record for this book is available from the British Library

ISBN 0-7463-1016-1 hardback
    0-7463-0908-2 paperback

Typeset by PDQ Typesetting, Newcastle-under-Lyme
Printed and bound in the United Kingdom by Athenaeum Press Ltd., Gateshead

KATHERINE MANSFIELD

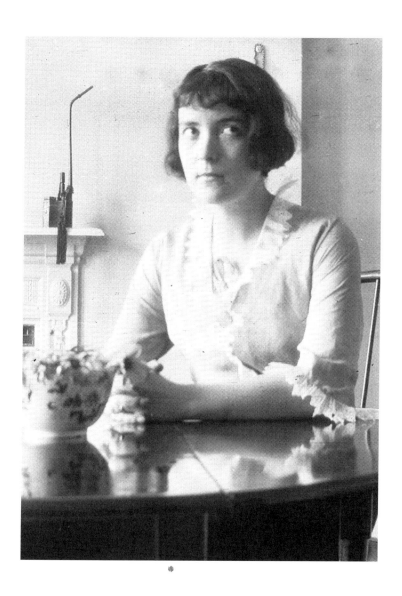

KATHERINE MANSFIELD

From a photograph, ca. 1913, of Katherine Mansfield at the Chaucer
Mansions flat, West Kensington, London, by Ida Constance Baker,
1888-1978. Reproduced by courtesy of the Ida Baker Collection,
Alexander Turnbull Library, Wellington, New Zealand (ref. F-59876-1/4).

Contents

Acknowledgements

I would like to thank my wife, Anna-Maria Hämäläinen-Bennett, for her support and encouragement during the writing of this book and for instructive and supportive comments on the project from her and from Isobel Armstrong, C. K. Stead and Angela Smith. The book was written in and near Lahti, Finland, in the summer of 2001, where I was particularly fortunate to be able to work in the secluded beauty of Salajärvi. I would like to thank Seppo and Pirjo Hämäläinen for their hospitality in allowing me to use their summer cottage, Salamyhkä, as a base for the writing of the book.

Parts of this book have been previously published in a different form in 'Hating Katherine Mansfield', *Angelaki* 7:3 (2002), 3–16.

Biographical Outline

1888   Born Kathleen Mansfield Beauchamp, 14 October at 11 Tinakori Road, Wellington, New Zealand.

1893   KM's family move to 'Chesney Wold', Karori.

1898   Father, Harold Beauchamp, appointed director of the Bank of New Zealand.

1903   Enters Queen's College, Harley Street, London, together with sisters, Vera and Chaddie; meets Ida Baker ('L.M.').

1906   October: returns to Wellington with family – first to 75 Tinakori Road and subsequently to 47 Fitzherbert Terrace.

1907   Harold Beauchamp appointed chairman of the Bank of New Zealand; KM's first mature pieces ('Vignettes' and 'Silhouettes') are published by the Melbourne-based *Native Companion*; KM takes part in a camping expedition into Urewera on the North Island.

1908   August: returns to London to stay in Beauchamp Lodge, Paddington.

1909   Marries George Bowden on 2 March and leaves him the same day; also leaves Beauchamp Lodge and travels with her lover, the musician Garnet Trowell, on tour in Glasgow and Liverpool; becomes pregnant; in May her mother arrives and takes her away to Bad Wörishofen in Bavaria before returning to New Zealand and cutting her daughter out of her will; KM subsequently miscarries; meets Floryan Sobieniowski, a Polish writer and translator with whom she falls in love and whom for a short time she plans to marry; returns to London after Christmas.

1910   First mature stories published in A. R. Orage's *New Age*; first signs of (undiagnosed) venereal disease; in March contracts peritonitis, is operated on and left fallopian tube is removed.

1911   December: *In a German Pension* published; meets the writer and critic John Middleton Murry.

1912   Murry moves in as KM's lodger and the two become lovers; KM's first publications in Murry's *Rhythm*.

1913   *Rhythm* becomes *Blue Review* but folds after three issues; KM and Murry begin friendship with D. H. Lawrence and Frieda; KM and Murry travel to Paris in December; KM meets Francis Carco.

1914   Return to London in February; Murry declared bankrupt; KM and Murry live in a number of cheap lodgings in London; in October they move to Great Missenden, near the Lawrences; KM unhappy in her relationship with Murry and begins an affair with Carco; writes only one story this year, 'Something Childish but very Natural'.

1915   KM begins 'The Aloe'; Leslie, KM's only brother, comes to England to enlist and is killed in France on 7 October; KM and Murry leave for Cassis and then Bandol in the south of France in November, Murry returning to London in December.

1916   KM Returns to England in the spring and from April to June lives with Murry next door to the Lawrences in Cornwall; meets Bertrand Russell, Virginia Woolf, and other members of the Bloomsbury circle.

1917   Rewrites 'The Aloe' as 'Prelude', to be published by the Hogarth Press in 1918; publishes several 'dialogues' ('Mr Reginald Peacock's Day', 'Feuille d'Album', and 'A Dill Pickle') in *New Age*; diagnosed with possible TB in December.

1918   Leaves for south of France in January on advice of doctor; has first haemorrhage of the lungs in February; returns to London via Paris in April; divorce from Bowden; KM and Murry married 3 May; *Prelude* published in July; KM's mother dies in August; KM writes 'Bliss', 'Je ne parle pas français'.

1919   Murry appointed editor of the *Athenaeum*, for which KM writes weekly reviews of novels; KM leaves for Italian Riviera in September on account of ill health; writes 'Psychology' but few other stories.

1920   In January travels to Menton; returns to London from April to September; in Menton writes 'The Man Without a Temperament', 'The Stranger', 'Miss Brill', 'The Daughters of the Late Colonel'; *Bliss and Other Stories* published in December.

1921   Leaves Menton for Switzerland in May, eventually settling in Montana-sur-Sierre; between August and October KM writes 'At the Bay', 'The Voyage', 'A Married Man's Story' (unfinished), 'The Garden Party', 'The Doll's House'.

1922   In January writes 'The Doves' Nest' (unfinished), 'A Cup of Tea', 'Taking the Veil'; leaves for Paris at the end of January to seek medical treatment; *The Garden Party and Other Stories* published in February; 'The Fly' published in March; returns to Switzerland in June; finishes her last completed story, 'The Canary', in July; returns briefly to London in August; travels to Paris in October and then on to George Gurdjieff's Institute for the Harmonious Development of Man at Fontainebleau.

1923   Dies on 9 January.

Abbreviations

CLKM *The Collected Letters of Katherine Mansfield*, ed. Vincent
      O'Sullivan and Margaret Scott, 4 vols. to date (Oxford:
      Clarendon Press, 1984–96)
CR   Jan Pilditch (ed.), *The Critical Response to Katherine
      Mansfield* (Westport, Conn.: Greenwood Press, 1996)
KMN   *The Katherine Mansfield Notebooks*, ed. Margaret Scott, 2
      vols. (Canterbury, NZ: Lincoln University Press, 1997)
L.   Antony Alpers, *The Life of Katherine Mansfield* (London:
      Jonathan Cape, 1980)
LKM   *The Letters of Katherine Mansfield*, ed. John Middleton
      Murry, 2 vols. (London: Constable, 1928)
SKM   *The Stories of Katherine Mansfield*, ed. Antony Alpers
      (Auckland: Oxford University Press, 1984)
SL   Claire Tomalin, *Katherine Mansfield: A Secret Life* (London:
      Penguin, 1988)
SS   *Selected Stories*, ed. Angela Smith (Oxford: Oxford Uni-
      versity Press, 2002)

Note on the Text

Mansfield's many spelling, grammar, and punctuation errors in quotations from the notebooks and letters have not been corrected. In the stories as well as in the notebooks and letters, Mansfield frequently used ellipses (...) as punctuation marks or rhetorical signs; where I have omitted words or phrases from a quotation this is indicated by square brackets around ellipses ([...]).

1

Introduction: A 'double life'

'There is no happiness greater than this leading a *double life*', Katherine Mansfield remarks on her life as a writer to the novelist William Gerhardie in June 1922. What Mansfield calls the 'mysterious' experience of writing involves being both 'here in this remote, deserted hotel' in Montana-sur-Sierre in Switzerland and at the same time 'in' the story she is writing, 'The Doves' Nest', a story set in a villa in the south of France. 'How is it possible to be here in this remote, deserted hotel', she asks, 'and at the same time to be leaning out of the window of the Villa Martin listening to the rain thrumming so gently on the leaves and smelling the night-scented stocks [...]' (*LKM* ii. 218). One of the most important short story writers in English, Mansfield may be said to have revolutionized her chosen form. Since her death in 1923, the reception of Mansfield's fictions has been bound up with her letters and notebooks and with accounts of her life. And yet many of the letters, notebooks, and stories are concerned to examine, in different ways, the complex relationship between writing and life, between story and autobiography, to examine the strangeness of the writer's 'double life', to ask the question: how is it possible to be here writing in this hotel and at the same time there, in the villa of fiction? This book focuses on Mansfield's 'double life', attempting to account for the relationship between Mansfield's life and her writing, and to examine that sense of the strange, the 'mysterious' nature of the act of writing.

Kathleen Mansfield Beauchamp was born on 14 October 1888 in Wellington, New Zealand. Her father, Harold Beauchamp, was a successful businessman who rose to become the chairman of the Bank of New Zealand. In 1903, at the age of 14, Mansfield was sent to England with her sisters to complete her education

1

in London, where at Queen's College she met Ida Baker, who was to become a lifelong friend and companion. She returned to New Zealand in December 1906 for eighteen months, during which time she had love affairs with at least two women and went on a formative month-long camping expedition in the Urewera region of the North Island. But Mansfield found her middle-class life in Wellington stifling and eventually persuaded her parents to allow her to return to London. In July 1908, at the age of 19, Mansfield set sail for England and was never again to visit her country of birth except in her dreams, in her memories, in her imagination, and, crucially, in some of her most well-known stories. Aside from a number of youthful stories published in school and college magazines, Mansfield's first publications – the sketches 'Vignette' and 'Silhouettes' – appeared in the Australian magazine *Native Companion* in October 1907. Writing to the editor in September with some 'details as to myself', Mansfield declared that she was 'poor – obscure – just eighteen years of age – with a rapacious appetite for everything and principles as light as my purse' (*CLKM* i. 26). Some of this, at least, seems to be borne out by the life that she created for herself on her return to London. As a young woman living independently in the capital with ambitions as, successively, a professional cellist, an actress, and a writer, Mansfield had affairs with a number of men, including George Bowden, whom she married and left the same day, and by her early twenties had managed to become pregnant, miscarry, and contract gonorrhoea. By now she had written and published a number of short stories – many for A. R. Orage's avant-garde literary magazine *New Age* – and in December 1911 she published her first collection of stories. *In a German Pension* is a collection of satirical tales based on Mansfield's experience of living in the spa town of Bad Wörishofen in Bavaria in 1909 during her pregnancy and her miscarriage and during a subsequent love affair with the Polish intellectual Floryan Sobieniowski. The caustic, often cynical book was relatively successful – not least, no doubt, because of its rather easy anti-German humour – and was reprinted three times before the publisher, Stephen Swift, went out of business. Later in life, however, Mansfield treated the book as a work of juvenilia and refused to allow it to be reprinted (it was only republished after her death). In 1910 she

2

sent 'The Woman at the Store', a New Zealand story based on her Urewera experiences, to John Middleton Murry, an aspiring writer and the editor of the literary journal *Rhythm*. Murry was impressed and published this and a number of other stories by Mansfield. She and Murry met at the end of 1911 and soon became lovers, living and working together in London, writing and editing *Rhythm*. On the fringes of the Bloomsbury circle, they were acquainted with some of the leading writers, intellectuals, and artists of the time – including Bertrand Russell, T. S. Eliot, E. M. Forster, Henri Gaudier-Brzeska, Lytton Strachey, Maynard Keynes, Aldous Huxley, and, most importantly, Virginia Woolf and D. H. Lawrence. As a 'colonial' from a family connected to commerce and as the mistress of the lower-middle-class Murry, however, Mansfield was always to remain on the fringes of this august grouping: as Elizabeth Bowen comments, amid the 'etherealities of Bloomsbury' Mansfield was 'more than half hostile'. In this company Mansfield was, according to Bowen, 'a dark-eyed tramp' (*CR* 74).

Between 1913, when *Rhythm* was forced to fold, and her death in January 1923 Mansfield lived in London, Cornwall, the French and the Italian Riviera, the Swiss Alps, and Paris, rarely settling for longer than a few months. For much of this time she was with Murry, whom she married in 1918 after Bowden had divorced her, but she often travelled and lived alone: Murry needed to be near London, where he continued to work as a critic and editor, and their relationship was often difficult and at times the couple became almost estranged. But throughout this time Mansfield was usually accompanied by her friend Ida Baker – 'L.M.' as Mansfield renamed her – who became Mansfield's selfless companion, helper, and even, in the writer's arguably non-sexual denomination, 'wife'. Mansfield's father gave her a modest allowance, but she and Murry, the poorly paid reviewer, editor, and aspiring writer, were rarely well off, at least until Murry's appointment to the editorship of the well-established and prestigious literary journal the *Athenaeum* in 1919. While their financial situation was itself part of the reason for the couple's somewhat nomadic lifestyle, more important was Mansfield's poor health and her need to spend winters in the milder Mediterranean climate. During the war years Mansfield was often ill as a result of undiagnosed gonorrhoea,

3

and she suffered from gonorrhoeal arthritis, infertility, heart problems, and repeated attacks of pleurisy. At some point, however, possibly as a result of her friendship with D. H. Lawrence, she contracted tuberculosis, which was eventually diagnosed in 1917. Her life from this time until her death was dominated by two strands in her writing – the development of innovative ways of telling stories, on the one hand, and the regular weekly hackwork of reviewing, on the other – and by the search for a cure for tuberculosis.

In 1915 Mansfield's younger brother Leslie had travelled to England to join up with the British army. His death in France in the summer was a severe blow to Mansfield, and, although Murry's often repeated idea that Leslie's death was responsible for his wife's creative breakthrough is probably more myth than reality,[1] there is from 1915 onwards an important return in her writing to her New Zealand childhood, a return that Mansfield herself suggests is payment for a 'sacred debt' to her own and her brother's homeland (*KMN* ii. 32). She soon began to write about those memories in a long story originally entitled *The Aloe*, which was later revised and published as *Prelude* by Leonard and Virginia Woolf's Hogarth Press. Despite her chronic ill health, Mansfield continued to work at the 'craft' of writing, eventually completing around ninety short stories and, in the process, transforming the genre. By the time she died in France at the age of 34 she had become a well-known and widely respected writer, had published numerous literary reviews, mostly for Murry's *Athenaeum*, and two more collections of stories – *Bliss and Other Stories* in 1920 and *The Garden Party and Other Stories* in 1922.

It was after her death, however, that Mansfield's publishing career and her reputation really took off, largely as a result of the efforts of her husband and literary executor, John Middleton Murry. After her death Murry published a collection of stories that Mansfield had been planning, *The Doves' Nest and Other Stories* (1923), and one more collection consisting of uncollected and unfinished stories, *Something Childish and Other Stories* (1924). Murry also republished Mansfield's first book, *In a German Pension*, and published a selection of her poems (1923), her *Journal* (1927), a two-volume selection of her letters (1928), a selection of her reviews, *Novels and Novelists* (1930), and a biography of her early life (1933; with Ruth Elvish Manzt). In 1939 he published a further selection of pieces from her notebooks entitled *The Scrapbook of Katherine Mansfield* and in 1951 an almost complete selection of her letters to himself. Finally, Murry put the *Journals* and the *Scrapbook* together as the so-called definitive edition of the *Journal* in 1954.

Mansfield's friendship with her fellow writer Virginia Woolf has received considerable critical attention in recent years[2] and Woolf's comments are a valuable source of information on her younger friend, providing important insights into Mansfield's 'double life', as a writer and as a woman. Woolf brings a novelist's observational powers to bear in her reactions to Mansfield. This close as well as often somewhat guarded relationship – at times intense, supportive, at times more wary, even jealous, founded, Woolf said, on 'quicksands'[3] – throws intriguing light on both women. Since both Woolf and Mansfield were writers, since both were attempting to forge a new language for fiction, since both were highly conscious of the relationship between gender and writing, and since both were, as Angela Smith comments, at the same time 'complicit with patriarchy and in opposition to it',[4] there was between the two women a certain amount of rivalry and even distrust combined with loyalty and mutual admiration. Between 1916 and 1920, Mansfield and Woolf met and corresponded many times, and they also had a professional relationship – Woolf publishing Mansfield's *Prelude* and Mansfield reviewing (with pronounced ambivalence) Woolf's novel *Night and Day* at least once and possibly twice, as well as a story prompted by Mansfield's own reflections in a letter to Woolf, *Kew Gardens*.[5] Woolf's initial reaction to Mansfield was imbued with a certain social snobbery combined with what seems to be a suspicion of the colonial: Katherine, she told her sister, is 'cheap and hard', 'unpleasant but forcible and utterly unscrupulous'.[6] This sense of distaste is redoubled in Woolf's sense of Mansfield's sexual licence: she has, Woolf declares 'gone every sort of hog since she was 17'. And yet Woolf's disapproval is immediately qualified by her assertion that it is Mansfield's unconventional life that makes her 'interesting'.[7] From the start, in fact, Woolf respected what she sensed as Mansfield's fierce commitment to the 'craft' of writing: Woolf noted in her diary, for example, that she felt a 'sense of ease' in Mansfield's presence, resulting from the fact that her friend cared 'so genuinely if so differently from the way I care, about our precious art'.[8] In another diary entry, from May 1920, Woolf records a visit in which she experienced from Mansfield 'a steady discomposing formality & coldness at first': 'It struck me that she is of the cat kind: alien, composed, always solitary & observant.' But at the same time, she hears Mansfield 'expressing my feelings, as I never heard them expressed',[9] and later comments that in Mansfield's presence she has 'the queerest sense of an echo coming back to me from her mind the second after I've spoken'.[10] What Woolf admires is Mansfield's passion for writing: 'A queer effect she produces of someone apart, entirely self-centred; altogether concentrated upon her "art": almost fierce to me about it.'[11] 'Her senses are amazingly acute,' Woolf writes, and there is, on her leaving, 'the blankness of not having her to talk to'.[12]

In 1931, eight years after Mansfield's death, Woolf wrote to Vita Sackville-West commenting on her friendship with Mansfield and on Mansfield's work. She remarks that she and Mansfield never really 'coalesced' – 'I thought her rather cheap, and she thought me priggish' – and that she, Woolf, had been 'jealous, no doubt' of her friend's literary powers and her critical success. Woolf's jealousy clearly affects her judgement of Mansfield's literary achievement, and is expressed in terms of a certain social distaste mixed up, no doubt, with a certain snobbery. In this respect, the letter tells us much about the social and literary contexts of Mansfield's life, about her experience of being a 'colonial' in London. Woolf's ambivalence towards Mansfield is expressed in her sense that her rival's stories have a certain 'cheap sharp sentimentality', and that their 'zest and [...] resonance' mean that Mansfield could 'permeate one with her quality'. But this 'quality' is itself ambiguous, since Woolf notes a 'cheap scent' in Mansfield's writing, which, she says, 'reeked in ones nostrils'. Once again, Woolf is both fascinated and appalled by what she sees as Mansfield's socially questionable lifestyle: 'I think her sharpness and reality – her having knocked about with prostitutes and so on, whereas I had always been respectable – was the thing I wanted then' she remarks. 'I dream of her often,' Woolf concludes, musing on how 'one's relation with a person seems to be continued after death in dreams, and with some odd reality too'.[13]

Perhaps Woolf's most important comments on Mansfield come in a diary entry dated 16 January 1923, written immediately after learning of her friend's death. Woolf provides a series of powerful – and powerfully ambivalent – insights into Mansfield's character and work, giving us a provocative account of her impressions of her fellow writer. Woolf records her sense of loss, her sense that she has lost both a literary peer and a literary rival. Sitting down to write, she says, she realizes that there is 'no point in writing', since 'Katherine wont read it', since 'Katherine's my rival no longer'. Out of this inability to write, though, Woolf articulates with an almost hallucinatory vividness her memory of their last meeting, in August 1920:

> And I could see her before me so exactly, & the room at Portland Villas. I go up. She gets up, very slowly, from her writing table. A glass of milk & a medicine bottle stood there. There were also piles of novels. Everything was very tidy, bright, & somehow like a dolls house. At once, or almost, we got out of shyness [...] She had her look of a Japanese doll, with the fringe combed quite straight across her forehead. Sometimes we looked very steadfastly at each other, as though we had reached some durable relationship, independent of the changes of the body, through the eyes. Hers were beautiful eyes – rather doglike, brown, very wide apart, with a steady slow rather faithful & sad expression. Her nose was sharp, & a little vulgar. Her lips thin & hard. She wore skirts & liked 'to have a line round her' she said. She looked very ill – very drawn, & moved languidly, drawing herself across the room, like some suffering animal [...] Most days I think we reached that kind of certainty, in talk about books, or rather about our writings, which I thought had something durable about it. And then she was inscrutable. Did she care for me? Sometimes she would say so – would kiss me – would look at me as if (is this sentiment?) her eyes would like always to be faithful [...] The surroundings – Murry & so on – & the small lies and treacheries, the perpetual playing & teasing, or whatever it was, cut away so much of the substance of friendship. One was too uncertain [...] And I was jealous of her writing – the only writing I have ever been jealous of. This made it harder to write to her; & I saw in it, perhaps from jealousy, all the qualities I disliked in her.[14]

This remarkably perceptive, painfully frank description encapsulates many of the reactions and the ambivalence that Woolf –

as well as others – felt towards Mansfield. While Woolf describes Mansfield's eyes as 'doglike' and her movements as those of an animal, she also notes a certain exotic role-playing in Mansfield's 'Japanese' hair, and records a sense of her as doll-like (both dolls and masks feature strongly in Mansfield's life and work). She is 'vulgar', tells 'small lies',[15] but is also flirtatious, she has a genuine sisterly empathy for Woolf, and has extraordinary and enviable literary powers. Both 'beautiful' and 'hard', 'vulgar' and 'languid', Mansfield provokes both sympathy – she moves 'like some suffering animal' – and jealousy. Woolf both dislikes her and feels that there is something 'durable' in their friendship. Mansfield likes to have 'a line drawn around her' and she is, finally, 'inscrutable'.[16]

In this book we will examine the inscrutability – the resistance to scrutiny – that encapsulates Mansfield for Woolf, and examine ways in which a certain inscrutability is inscribed in Mansfield's writing – in her journals, letters, and fictions and in the relationship between the two parts of her 'double life', between her life and her writing. If, as I have suggested, the assessment of Mansfield's work has been bound up since her death with assessments of her life, this is the case not least because of Murry's efforts to publish her letters and notebooks, her poems and scraps of writing, and her biography. Only now, almost 80 years after her death, is an accurate picture of that life and work becoming available, with the publication of scholarly editions of Mansfield's letters and notebooks – itself the major development in Mansfield studies of the final decades of the twentieth century. Four of the five volumes of the definitive *Collected Letters of Katherine Mansfield*, edited by Vincent O'Sullivan and Margaret Scott, appeared between 1984 and 1996, and Margaret Scott's authoritative edition of the notebooks was published in 1997. These editions allow us to take a new look at Mansfield's 'double life', at the relationship between her life and her writing, and between different kinds of writing that she accomplished – reviews, diaries, notebooks, and letters as well as stories. And they also allow us to escape from the perhaps rather falsified, romanticized image of Mansfield presented in the decades after her death by Murry, whose publication of edited, revised, and selected versions of the letters and notebooks included countless editorial decisions that often seem to have more to do with his own somewhat idealistic, even mystical notion of Art and Literature than with hers.[17] What becomes clear from the full texts of the letters, notebooks, and stories is that central to Mansfield's writing and to her life is precisely the question of the relationship between writing and life, between art and personality, between form and passion. In this book we will examine Mansfield's major achievement, the evolution – or even revolution – that she effected in the form of short fiction as a development bound up with her sense of personality, of personhood, of impersonality and impersonation – bound up, in the end, with Mansfield's own mobile, fractured, and multiple sense of personal identity.

2

'This secret disruption': Katherine Mansfield's Identities

In October 1922, only months before her death and after years of chronic illness, years of fruitless and sometimes cranky medical treatment, years of physical pain, and years of what amounts to denial – denial of the seriousness of her condition and of her prospects for a long life – Mansfield wrote to her friend S. S. Koteliansky ('Kot') of her decision to stop seeking medical treatment and instead to retreat to George Gurdjieff's Institute for the Harmonious Development of Man at Fontainebleau. In this letter, as in others written at around this time, Mansfield expresses her belief that she is breaking with the past and making a new beginning. She writes of her sense of having lived a double life, of being 'superficial' not only in relation to others but also in relation to herself, and of her sense that, as she writes to Kot, 'I am always conscious of this secret disruption in me' (*LKM* ii. 260). In a letter to Murry written two days later, she returns to the theme and to her 'secret sorrow' that she has 'always been', in the 'deepest sense', 'disunited' (*LKM* ii. 261).

While Mansfield presents this as a new awakening, a new perception of her spiritual state, in fact from the start of her writing life her writing and her life were built on and built around such a 'secret disruption' – around a sense of the fragility, the mobility, and the multiplicity of personal identity. Highly conscious of personality as a mask, role, or performance, Mansfield inscribes this sense of the constructedness of the self, of personal identity, in her published and unpublished prose. According to her long-term friend and companion Ida Baker, Mansfield was a 'born actress and mimic',[1] and critics have long recognized that the key to Mansfield's life as well as to her literary achievement is a certain strategy of impersonation. Brigid Brophy comments, for example, that Mansfield's 'obvious – indeed, dazzling – talent is for multiple impersonation' (CR 90), and Sydney Kaplan remarks that Mansfield's narrative poetics are 'grounded in a precocious recognition of the self as many selves'.[2] One of the simplest ways in which Mansfield articulated a sense of fracturing and multiplicity in her personality was by naming and renaming herself. Christened Kathleen Mansfield Beauchamp, her name was changed by marriage, first to Katherine Bowden in 1909 and then to Katherine Mansfield Murry in 1918. But it seems that none of her three official names was particularly important to her, and throughout her life she gave herself different names in different contexts and for different people. Her adopted names, pet names, and pen names included the name by which she is now universally known and which she adopted soon after her return to England in 1908, Katherine Mansfield, as well as a host of others: Kätherine Schönfeld, Julian Mark, Karl Mansfield, Käthe Beauchamp-Bowden, Yekaterina, Katerina Mansfield, K. M. Beauchamp, K. Mansfield, K.M., K.T., Kath, Lili Heron, Sally, The Tiger, Tig, Katya, Katy Mansfield, Kissienka, Katie, Katiushka, Elizabeth Stanley, Catherina, Kass – and even, disconcertingly, Boris Petrovsky.[3] One of her friends from her early London years felt that with each name Mansfield would 'assume another personality',[4] and a change of name was often accompanied by a change of appearance, including even a change in her ethnic or national identity – Maori, for example, or Japanese or Russian or French. As Angela Smith comments, these changes in identity seem to imply an 'awareness of multiple selves, and perhaps of the difficulty of deciding what aspect of the "soul" to reflect' in the way that she presented herself to the world.[5] Her first husband, George Bowden, clearly baffled by a woman who could marry him and leave him on the same day, was convinced that differences in appearance denoted not just an 'impersonation' but what he called a 'psychic transformation' (L. 87). As Brigid Brophy puts it of this 'polymorphous poseuse', Mansfield was 'in the habit of running up spare personalities for herself' (CR 89). As a consequence of this habit, both contemporaries and later readers and critics have been uncertain, troubled even by her identities, by how to categorize her. Listing the different 'Katherine Mansfields' that have been written about since her death, one critic gives a sense of this confusing, often contradictory, multiplicity: her identity has been construed as that of a 'supersensitive female', an 'immoral woman', a 'tubercular victim', an 'acid-tongued shrew', a 'colonial *naïve*', a 'boring imitator', an 'absorbing innovator', a 'feminist reformer', a 'secret lesbian', a 'social climber', a 'plagiarist', a 'sloppy sentimentalist', an 'arch satirist', and so on.[6]

From the age of 17, Katherine Mansfield regularly wrote in a series of notebooks, recording drafts of stories and letters, critical commentaries, personal impressions, quotations, reading notes, household jottings, diary entries, and endless self-reflections. The notebooks are an intimate and often remarkable record of her thoughts, ideas, inspirations, obsessions, desires, hatreds, passions. Sometimes they were written as a diary recording her life, but more often Mansfield used them as a kind of scrapbook to record her impressions of people and places, her ideas for drafts of stories, her thoughts on life and on literature, her developing sense of the proper structure for 'modern' narratives, and her ambitions for and sense of herself. Together with the letters, the notebooks provide fascinating insights into Mansfield's life and writing. In particular, they record two recurrent concerns: Mansfield's thoughts on writing and fiction and her developing sense of her self or selves. From their first, partial publication by John Middleton Murry soon after her death, the letters and notebooks have been valued – like Keats's letters, which, as Murry almost obsessively emphasized, they often seem to echo – for their very informality, for the scrappiness and the heterogeneity of their subject matter, for the way that a glancing, offhand comment on literature or life of great interest and significance will be thrown off amongst the trivia of everyday concerns. As C. K. Stead comments, in the letters and journals Mansfield 'lays before us as few writers have done, the psychic state, the inner condition, of the artist whose material is language'.[7]

In this chapter I want to focus on a number of passages in the letters and notebooks that explore the nature of the self, of the multiple selves that Mansfield constructs and performs. This multiplicity, heterogeneity, and instability in Mansfield's sense of selfhood is, I will suggest, central to her writing. In this respect, the originality of Mansfield's stories lies in their relation to the development of her technique of 'impersonation', a term that might indicate both a removal of the 'person' of the writer from the text, a removal of authorial commentary, and an impersonation of narratorial and characterological voices, an acting-out of or playing on characters' voices as the motive force of narrative form. The notebooks and letters give a powerful sense of the development of Mansfield's concern with personality, impersonality, and impersonation.

In two early notebook entries Mansfield struggles with the twin concerns – of narrative form and personal identity – that are to dominate her mature work. In the first, an entry dated 21 December 1908, written when Mansfield was just 20 years old, she contemplates writing a story about a young woman like herself in the style of Walter Pater's *Child in the House*:

> I should like to write a life . . . About a girl in Wellington; the singular charm and barrenness of that place, with climatic effects – wind, rain, spring, night, the sea, the cloud pageantry. And then to leave the place and go to Europe, to live there a dual existence – to go back and be utterly disillusioned, to find out the truth of all, to return to London. to live there an existence so full & so strange that Life itself seemed to greet her, and, ill to the point of death, return to W. & die there. A story, no, it would be a sketch, hardly that, more a psychological study of the most erudite character. I should fill it with climatic disturbance, & also of the strange longing for the artificial. I should call it 'Strife', & the child I should call – Ah, I have it – I'd make her a half caste Maori & call her Maata. (*KMN* i. 111)

This early and, as one critic calls it, 'eerily prescient' notebook entry, is resonant with themes from Mansfield's own life and from her own writing.[8] She too is a 'girl in Wellington' who leaves to go to Europe, who then returns disillusioned to New Zealand, before travelling once more, and permanently, back to Europe and London. Towards the end of her life Mansfield too yearned to return to New Zealand, but in 1908 she had no way of knowing that she would never again return to her country of birth. The passage expresses the ambivalence that Mansfield feels towards New Zealand itself, a place with both a 'singular charm' and an irreducible 'barrenness'. The summary dwells,

13

characteristically, on the scenery of New Zealand and its 'climatic disturbance' as well as on the girl's subsequent disillusionment and on the 'strangeness' of London. It fantasizes about a life lived to the 'full' and about illness and death in ways clearly influenced not only by Pater but also by her literary hero of the time, Oscar Wilde. 'Strange' – used twice in this passage – is an important word throughout Mansfield's writing life, and, linked with both 'longing' and the Wildean notion of the 'artificial', it constitutes a continuing motif in her work. And the passage ends in an intriguing reference to and identification with New Zealand's cultural others, Maoris, inspired, as her choice of name makes clear, by her schoolfriend and lover Maata Mahupuka. Most importantly, however, the passage allows us to observe the young Mansfield attempting to work out a mode of writing that goes beyond what she sees as the limitations of the literary and novelistic conventions of the early twentieth century, struggling to develop a new form of writing to express her semi-articulated longings: 'A story, no, it would be a sketch, hardly that, more a psychological study of the most erudite character.' Working on it, working it out as she writes, Mansfield gives us a remarkable insight into her early sense of the inadequacies of the available critical and conceptual vocabularies. While her reputation as a writer is based on her production of short stories, her narratives are often no more than 'sketches': many were incomplete, but even the finished stories often lack the narrative impetus, the concatenation of event and incident, the temporal and logical sequence of linear progression that we expect from narrative, with its characterological development and comforting resolution or 'closure'. Indeed, as Mansfield herself seems to sense in this notebook, the stories that she is to write might often be more properly defined as 'psychological studies' than stories or even sketches.

In a slightly earlier notebook entry written during her return to New Zealand from December 1906 to August 1908, Mansfield gives further evidence of her early sense of the limitations of conventional narrative form and links it to her preoccupation with personal identity. In this entry Mansfield makes a revealing comparison between what might be conceived even at this early date as the psychoanalytical or Freudian perspective on character and her own – an opposition that she characterizes as between 'partisans of analysis', on the one hand, and 'partisans of objectivity' on the other:

> The partisans of analysis describe minutely the state of the soul, the secret motive of every action as being of far greater importance than the action itself. The partisans of objectivity give us the result of this evolution sans describing the secret processes. They convey the state of the soul through the slightest gesture – i.e. realism, flesh covered bones, which is also the artists method for me. In as much as art seems to me *pure vision* I am indeed a partisan of objectivity. Yet I cannot take the simile of the soul and the body for the bone is no bony framework. Supposing ones bones were not bone but liquid light – which suffuses itself, fluctuates – well and good, but the bones are permanent and changeless – [therefore] – that fails. (*KMN* i. 156)

The passage is again remarkably prescient in its conception of Mansfield's future writing career and again reveals Mansfield struggling – and failing – to work out an adequate vocabulary to describe her work. One of the things that marks Mansfield's mature stories is the way that they appeal to but finally resist psychological or psychoanalytic analysis or commentary, the way that they hint at but also diverge from any appeal to or investigation of the unconscious. Mansfield's work is remarkable, not least, for the extent of her restraint, restraint in the first place of authorial commentary on issues of psychological motivation. Mansfield effectively transforms the short story and does so, in part, by a refusal to define an origin – an explanation – for peoples' actions or a 'secret' core of personality. Her interest is in the superficial, one might say, whereby an analysis of 'secret processes' is largely eschewed and representation limited to what she terms the 'objective' aspects of character – people's dress, mannerisms, speech patterns, habits, and so on. And her resistance to the metaphor of bone and flesh is also revealing, since the substitution of hard, 'changeless' bones by 'liquid light', with its quality of 'suffusing' and 'fluctuating', is suggestive of Mansfield's often frustrated attempt to escape from the rigid linear structure of conventional narrative form, and from the fixities and certainties of characterological definition. Mansfield's best writing may be said to be characterized by a 'suffusing' and 'fluctuating' perception and perspective.

But if Mansfield's poetics are concerned with the mobility and fluidity of narrative perspective, with an interest in the superficial, with appearances and surfaces, it is clear that such a concern stems from Mansfield's own sense of self, of herself. As I have suggested, an abiding concern of her writing, and of her letters and journals, is the question of the nature of the self, of writing about the self and of the relationship between self and others. In a later but equally remarkable notebook entry from 1920, Mansfield returns to her concern with the nature of the self and gives a richer, more nuanced sense of the complications of the question. Irritated by the way that the Shakespearian motto 'To thine own self be true' is endlessly and unthinkingly repeated in fashionable autograph albums of the late nineteenth and early twentieth centuries, Mansfield works out a different, even paradoxical notion of selfhood:

> True to oneself! Which self? Which of my many – well, really, that's what it looks like coming to – hundreds of selves. For what with complexes and suppressions, and reactions and vibrations and reflections – there are moments when I feel I am nothing but the small clerk of some hotel without a proprietor who has all his work cut out to enter the names and hand the keys to the wilful guests. (*KMN* ii. 204)

Mansfield's assertion of the multiplicity of the self and its lack of 'agency' (the hotel-owner does not exist and his place is taken by a functionary) is characteristic of her challenge to conventional notions of personal identity. The comments incorporate both a 'Freudian' sense of 'complexes and suppressions', and a rather different, more superficial, vaguer, more flexible sense of the importance of 'reactions and vibrations and reflections'. But the passage does not end here and goes on to suggest that the modern era is peculiarly concerned with locating and defining the individual subject, with defining the self:

> Nevertheless, there are signs that we are intent as never before on trying to puzzle out, to live by, our own particular self. *Der mensch muss frei sein* – free, disentangled, single. Is it not possible that the rage for confession, autobiography, especially for memories of earliest childhood is explained by our persistent yet mysterious belief in a self which is continuous and permanent, which, untouched by all we acquire and all we shed, pushes a green spear through the leaves and through the mould, thrusts a sealed bud through years of

16

darkness until, one day, the light discovers it and shakes the flower free and – we are alive – we are flowering for our moment upon the earth. This is the moment which, after all, we live for, the moment of direct feeling when we are most ourselves and least personal. (*KMN* ii. 204)

In this passage Mansfield allows for a balancing of her scepticism towards the individual – towards the autonomous, single, authentic self – by suggesting the importance of the drive towards self-definition. In beautifully cadenced prose, she leads up to the conclusion that there is a 'self' independent of history, circumstances, life experience. But the passage as a whole, with its consideration and deployment of two opposing positions, enacts the tension between two conflicting notions of the self – the self as multiple and the self as unique, individual, permanent. And the note ends in a careful balancing of the two arguments, a kind of reconciliation of the difference expressed in the paradoxical formula 'most ourselves and least personal', which emphasizes the contradiction contained within the notion of the unique, personal self: when we are 'most ourselves' we are also 'least personal', because this flowering self has nothing to do with personality, with the will, with the person of ourself. This complex notion of selfhood, of the multiplicity and individuality of the self, is played out in Mansfield's stories and in her writing practice. Interestingly, it is also played out in the critical responses to her writing, from the very first reviews onwards. Mansfield's writing poses the question of the extent to which her 'personality' is embedded within or constituted by her writing. In a review of *The Garden Party and Other Stories*, for example, Conrad Aiken suggests that Mansfield's technique involves 'ventriloquistic feats' in which she speaks as different people. As his somewhat pejorative use of 'ventriloquism' would suggest, for Aiken Mansfield's writing is limited by the fact that characters speak in the end 'with her voice', that they 'think as she thinks': instead of 'submerging herself in her characters', he declares, Mansfield 'submerges her characters in herself' (*CR* 10–11). But in a review of *The Doves' Nest and Other Stories* by Raymond Mortimer exactly the opposite point is made and Mansfield is criticized for precisely the opposite limitation. Mortimer suggests that Mansfield's stories are written in what he calls 'oratorio obliqua', a method that makes it 'extraordinarily difficult to discover the real colour of the author's mind', and that thereby prevents Mansfield from developing 'that affectionate relationship of reader to author which ties us to many of the great writers of the past' (*CR* 13). The achievement – and the difficulty, the risk even – of Mansfield's major work is encapsulated in the way that the two critics produce contrasting responses to the problem of Mansfield's identities and to what we might call her poetics of impersonation.

A certain impersonality was the ideal that Mansfield strove for in her writing, although for her – as for T. S. Eliot rather differently in his sense of the 'impersonality' of the poet[9] – impersonality is bound up in the question of impersonation. In a notebook entry from 1921, the concern with narrative and its form comes together with Mansfield's interest in the nature of personal identity. She wonders why she cannot be more humble and why she repeatedly discovers that she is 'preening' herself on completing a story. 'This interferes very much with work', she remarks:

> One can't be calm, clear, good as one must be while it goes on. I look at the mountains, I try to pray, & I think of something *clever*. It's a kind of excitement within one which shouldn't be there. Calm yourself. Clear yourself. And anything that I write in this mood will be no good; it will be full of *sediment*. If I were well I would go off by myself somewhere & sit under a tree. One must learn, one must practice to forget oneself. I can't tell the truth about Aunt Anne unless I am free to enter into her life without selfconsciousness. Oh God! I am divided still. I am bad. I fail in my personal life. I lapse into impatience, temper, vanity & so I fail as thy priest. Perhaps poetry will help. (*KMN* ii. 296)

Once again, the passage not only argues but also plays out or performs its concern with paradoxical, conflicted ideas of the self, once again producing an unstable, paradoxical balancing of the impersonal, the dispassionate, with the personal, the impassioned. The conflicted nature of the passage is suggested not least in its closing words, where a certain voice is impersonated, a certain rhetoric adopted – where Mansfield deploys the religious, devotional language of prayer. Paradoxically, Mansfield argues for *impersonality* by giving voice to the intensely *personal* mode of the subject in prayer: one of

Mansfield's multiple voices, multiple impersonations, is that of intense personal articulation, even, as here, in an argument for impersonality. In this passage, then, Mansfield performs the paradox, the dilemma, of personality that dominates her writing – her sense that egoism is undesirable and that the artist needs to develop a certain impersonality but that impersonality might include the impersonation of personality, of passion. The modernist notion of the impersonality of the poet is compromized and complicated here and elsewhere by Mansfield's impersonation, impersonation that both articulates an evacuation of the self and produces a personal voice, produces a person.

This struggle between the 'personal' and the impersonal, between personality and impersonation, is a continuing theme in Mansfield's letters and notebooks and is developed variously in her short stories. At times it is connected to her recurrent sense of despair and to her chronic illnesses. 'At the back of my mind I am so wretched,' she remarks in one journal entry, 'but all the while I am thinking over my philosophy – the defeat of the personal' (*KMN* ii. 190). The 'defeat of the personal' amounts to a certain 'philosophy', but more importantly perhaps it amounts to a certain aesthetics, contributing as it does to the production, over a lifetime, of Mansfield's narrative poetics and to her characteristic mode of writing. But the theory of what Eliot calls 'impersonality' and of what critics tend to refer to as 'impersonation' in Mansfield's work is most clearly expressed in a letter to Murry dated 3 November 1920. In this letter, as on other occasions, Mansfield echoes Keats's sense of the poet as 'chameleon':[10] 'What a QUEER business writing is' she declares in a passage that silently invokes a story, 'The Stranger', that she had completed the previous day:

> 'Ive *been* this man *been* this woman. Ive stood for hours on Auckland Wharf. Ive been out in the stream waiting to be berthed. Ive been a seagull hovering at the stern and a hotel porter whistling through his teeth. It isn't that one sits and watches the spectacle. That would be thrilling enough, God knows. But one IS the spectacle for the time [...] It's a lightning change affair [...]   (*CLKM* iv. 97)

This sense of identification with the 'spectacle', this 'lightning change affair', is, indeed, embedded within the texture of

19

Mansfield's very prose as a form of linguistic impersonation. In the stories, Mansfield is not just interested in *imagining* the consciousness of another but in *writing* that consciousness, in inscribing it in language. It is for this reason that her stories often seem particularly resistant to critical analysis: the authorial voice is submerged into the voice of the character him- or herself, and these fluid, unstable identifications give the reader or critic little purchase on a governing or authorial identity.

Mansfield's concerns with impersonality and impersonation in her letters and notebooks come together in a remarkable passage from another letter written two months later (dated 17 January 1921). In this letter, Mansfield dwells on the 'craft' of writing, the craft, that is, of writing in the voice of another, in this case that of Miss Brill:

> Its a very queer thing how craft comes into writing. I mean down to details. Par exemple. In Miss Brill I chose not only the length of every sentence, but even the sound of every sentence – I chose the rise and fall of every paragraph to fit her – and to fit her on that day at that very moment. After Id written it I read it aloud – numbers of times – just as one would *play over* a musical composition, trying to get it nearer and nearer to the expression of Miss Brill – until it fitted her. (*CLKM* iv. 165)

The letter gives a fine sense of the work involved in Mansfield's writing, and of the extent to which her 'craft' is embodied in the tone, the rhythm, the lexical details of her language – language that is not so much hers as that of her characters. The very materials that she uses – her words – become other to the writer, become those of another being. As the letter continues, Mansfield's sense of this 'queer' craft is elaborated into an argument about modernism more generally. She suggests a future for prose and argues that people are constituted more by what is not known about them than by what is:

> people have hardly begun to write yet [...] I mean prose. Take the very best of it. Aren't they still cutting up sections rather than tackling the whole of a mind? I had a moment of absolute terror in the night. I suddenly thought of *a living mind* – a whole mind – with absolutely nothing left out. With *all* that one knows how much does one *not* know? I used to fancy one knew all but some kind of mysterious core (or one could). But now I believe just the opposite. The unknown is far greater than the known. The known is only a

mere shadow. This is a fearful thing and terribly hard to face. But it must be faced. (*CLKM* iv. 165)

Mansfield here articulates a conventional sense of personality as having hidden depths, as being structured or determined by 'secrets'. But she also suggests a resistance to the conventional, reductive sense of the unconscious as somehow accessible or recoverable, of the 'secrets' of personality as decodable. What is terrifying to her is the sense that a 'whole mind' is determined by what is unknown and unknowable – terrifying not least because it challenges fundamentally the central beliefs of the so-called humanist notion of selfhood, including the idea that one's own mind is ultimately knowable. The point is 'fearful' and 'terribly hard to face' because of our investment in the possibility of personal insight, of self-consciousness or self-awareness and of volition, of the power to decide, to choose, to act. And, of course, Mansfield also realizes that she has presented herself with an impossible, paradoxical task as a writer, the task of 'facing' the human truth of the self as unknowable: she presents herself with the task of writing the unknown, with articulating the 'living mind' as, pre-eminently, that which cannot be known, cannot be articulated.

3

'Hesitations, doubts, beginnings'

In a letter dated 24 June 1922, Katherine Mansfield writes to an aspiring novelist Arnold Gibbons advising him on the stories that he has sent her for her comments. She tells Gibbons that his stories are 'awfully good' but that they don't 'quite come off' because, she says, 'you used more words than were necessary. There's a kind of diffuseness of expression,' she continues, 'which isn't natural to the English way of thinking' (*LKM* ii. 220). And she contrasts Gibbons's 'diffuseness' with the elliptical compression of Chekhov – Gibbons's, as well as Mansfield's own literary model. Mansfield then cites some examples of this diffuseness – essentially a kind of loquacious and repetitive vapidity of expression – and comments that 'When one writes like that in English it's as though the *nerve* of the feeling were gone'. 'I realise it's all very well to say these things,' continues Mansfield, as if talking to herself, 'but how are we going to convey these overtones, half tones, quarter tones, these hesitations, doubts, beginnings, if we go at them *directly*. It is most devilishly difficult, but I do believe that there is a way of doing it and that's by trying to get as near to the *exact truth* as possible' (*LKM* ii. 221–2).

This chapter considers ways in which Mansfield's work is concerned with indirection and with the expression of the 'truth' of 'overtones, half tones, quarter tones [...] hesitations, doubts, beginnings', with the representation of experiences, thoughts, emotions – even actions and events – by allusion, suggestion, inference, and implication, by the articulation of the gaps between words, in other words, by silence and restraint, by a certain compression, and by the avoidance of 'diffuseness' and repetition: by not saying what is said. As Vincent O'Sullivan has suggested, Mansfield's prose is characterized by 'indirections, shifts of perspective, overlappings of minds, modulations of time, careful imprecisions of moods' and 'painstaking randomness' (*CR* 140).[1] The difficulty of this new kind of writing – the difficulty of writing it – is expressed in a letter addressed to Dorothy Brett dated 25 July 1921: 'Oh, Heavens – how difficult Art is. It's the perpetual work at technique which is so hard. Its not enough to know what you want to say – but to be able to say it – to be equipped to say it! That's a life's work' (*CLKM* iv. 255).

Mansfield had, she told Virginia Woolf, a 'passion for writing' (*CLKM* ii. 314). The phrase involves an ambiguous sense of the object of this passion, leaving it uncertain whether she is referring to the act of writing or to literary texts themselves. Both come together, however, in Mansfield's passion for a new or renewed mode of writing – in what she later calls her 'passion for technique', out of which is born 'real style': 'There are no short cuts', she declares (*CLKM* iv. 173). The desire to write a new kind of prose, the sense that a new kind of writing was possible, was central to Mansfield's reflections on her own work. 'People have never explored the lovely medium of prose', she comments in a letter concerning Joyce's just-published *Ulysses*: like death in *Hamlet* and like New Zealand in another context, prose is, she thinks, 'a hidden country still' (*CLKM* ii. 343).[2] In a passage from a letter quoted at the end of Chapter 2, Mansfield contemplates the work involved in writing the voice of the eponymous Miss Brill: 'In Miss Brill I chose not only the length of every sentence, but even the sound of every sentence – I chose the rise and fall of every paragraph to fit her – and to fit her on that day at that very moment. After Id written it I read it aloud – numbers of times – just as one would *play over* a musical composition, trying to get it nearer and nearer to the expression of Miss Brill – until it fitted her' (*CLKM* iv. 165). As we have seen, the technique that Mansfield is describing here – that of 'impersonation' – itself demands a certain restraint, the eschewal, in particular, of authorial or narratorial commentary. 'Impersonation' demands that 'truth' is expressed through allusion, inference, and indirection, and Mansfield's contribution to the development of the short story in English may be said to be defined most of all in terms of this restraint of commentary.

The difficulty, the risk involved in Mansfield's technique of impersonation, in the merging of narrative or authorial voice into the voices of characters, is that it is, by definition, open to misinterpretation. Mansfield's technique is constitutively resistant to interpretation to the extent that interpretation depends on the possibility of a stable, identifiable origin, a source of speech or of writing. Mansfield's 'art' involves precisely the indirection that she talks about in her letter to Arnold Gibbons, an indirection that involves both a *lack* of direction and a certain *mis*direction. This is a difficulty, as Mansfield makes clear, of writing, but it is also of course a difficulty in reading, in interpretation. Reading becomes risky, since the reader is impelled to make judgements without the information necessary for those judgements. Again and again, for example, Mansfield's stories begin *in medias res* and with no indication of the status of the language used, its origin, its 'author'. One of her best-known and most anthologized stories, 'Bliss', for example, opens by throwing the reader into the middle of the story, and making her interpret against rather than with the speech patterns of its main character. But it is only on rereading that we are aware how much the very diction and syntax, the very rhetorical and figurative dimensions of language, are themselves provoking us towards an oppositional reading:

> Although Bertha Young was thirty she still had moments like this when she wanted to run instead of walk, to take dancing steps on and off the pavement, to bowl a hoop, to throw something up in the air and catch it again, or to stand still and laugh at – nothing – at nothing, simply.
>
>   What can you do if you are thirty and, turning the corner of your own street, you are overcome, suddenly, by a feeling of bliss – absolute bliss! – as though you'd suddenly swallowed a bright piece of that late afternoon sun and it burned in your bosom, sending out a little shower of sparks into every particle, into every finger and toe?... (*SS* 174)

Young at 30, Bertha's gushing enthusiasm for life is expressed in the accretive syntax of the first paragraph, by the emptily bombastic repetitions of both 'laugh at – nothing – at nothing' and 'a feeling of bliss – absolute bliss! –', by the vacuous rhetorical question and significant dots of the second paragraph, and by its extraordinary mixed metaphor of swallowing, burning, and sparking. But these satirical figurative and syntactical features only indirectly tell us what we need to know – that Bertha's state of mind is unstable, indeed approaching the hysterical and delusional. What the opening paragraphs of 'Bliss' also do – not least with the inclusive 'we' – is to encourage the reader to identify with and feel sympathy for this state of heightened awareness, this state of 'bliss'.

As the story continues, the gap between Bertha's blissful sense of life's possibilities and the reality are indirectly indicated – indicated precisely by impersonating this enthusiasm – well before the abrupt denouement of the ending reveals the extent of her delusion. The narrative trajectory of 'Bliss', that is to say, is revealed at the end to have been encoded within the prose from the story's opening sentence. Bertha's blissful satisfaction with her life is presented in the pointed, satirical phrasing of Mansfield's impersonation, which both expresses and undercuts that satisfaction at the same time:

> Really – really – she had everything. She was young. Harry and she were as much in love as ever, and they got on together splendidly and were really good pals. She had an adorable baby. They didn't have to worry about money. They had this absolutely satisfactory house and garden. And friends – modern, thrilling friends, writers and painters and poets or people keen on social questions – just the kind of friends they wanted. And then there were books, and there was music, and she had found a wonderful little dressmaker, and they were going abroad in the summer, and their new cook made the most superb omelettes . . . (SS 178)

The vacuousness and superficiality of Bertha's desires and satisfactions are paradoxically expressed, unwittingly, by Bertha herself in the phrasings and the self-contradictions of the paragraph: she and her husband are 'as much in love as ever' but also 'pals'; Bertha has little access to her 'adorable' baby, who is mainly looked after by a nurse; the hyperbole of her blissful state is exposed for what it is in the verbal tension of the quasi-oxymoronic phrase 'absolutely satisfactory'; Bertha's friends are valued more for their 'modernity' than for their personalities; 'books', 'music', and 'abroad' remain suspiciously unspecific; and, despite Bertha's satisfaction, the new cook's major achievement appears to be sadly limited to the production of omelettes ('the most superb omelettes' is again something like an oxymoron: in the end, an omelette is an omelette). Mansfield's commentary on her character, then, is indirectly suggested by the character's own words, which undercut Bertha's sense of her self in a way that she articulates but fails to understand.

Indirection also plays a crucial part in 'The Voyage', where a very different effect – pathos rather than satire – is produced by Mansfield's impersonation of the main character. The story is told from the perspective of a young girl, Fenella, who is travelling from Wellington on the North Island to Picton on the South Island. She is travelling with her grandmother, and will be staying with her grandparents for an unspecified length of time. She says goodbye to her father, goes on board, enters the cabin with her grandmother and goes to sleep in the bunk bed. When she wakes the ship has arrived at its destination and she and her grandmother travel on to the house where her grandfather is in bed awaiting her arrival. Such a summary does little to explain a story in which all interest is focused on the question of understanding, of how meanings come to be understood. The story is concerned not so much with narrative revelation or with what happened to Fenella as with the process of understanding what happened. The reader's grasp of events is restricted by the fact that we are privileged to witness only what Fenella herself witnesses, and her understanding is limited by her youth. The dynamic of the story – its eventfulness, in effect – is focused around the distinction between what Fenella makes of her journey and what we make of her understanding. It is only gradually, as the story unfolds, that we start to understand that the narrative is concerned with unbearable and for Fenella hardly realized grief at her mother's death. As her father takes leave of her grandmother, for example, Fenella is surprised and disturbed by his emotion and by her grand-mother's tears. Since Fenella herself does not acknowledge the reason for this emotion, the reader is also unaware of its cause, and it is only Fenella's resistance to her own emotion that suggests how deeply she is affected: 'This was so awful that Fenella quickly turned her back on them, swallowed once, twice, and frowned terribly at a little green star on a mast head' (SS 316). The black clothes that Fenella and her grandmother wear, certain comments by her grandmother and the stewardess, her grandmother's insistent tact and prayerfulness all point to the fact that Fenella's mother has recently died and that all the things that draw Fenella's attention – these black clothes themselves, her grandmother's umbrella, the eye-like porthole, the stars, the details of the ship, and her grandparents' house – are objects that distract her attention from what we come to realize is an unbearable burden of grief, an inconsolable sorrow. The story concerns the inability of the child to experience this grief, even fully to understand its source – her mother's death, her own effective orphanhood – and is focused around the discrepancy between her appalling loss and her inability fully to conceptualize, even to experience it. By limiting her perspective to that of the child – by impersonating Fenella's own sense of things – Mansfield not only explores this discrepancy, but enacts it for the reader, making the reader experience something of the emotional dislocation that is Fenella's own condition.

A major dimension of Mansfield's work concerns the difficulty of relationships and the isolation, often the loneliness of the individual, and her fictions often revolve around difficult, stalled, failed or failing, disfunctional and miscomprehending conversations. 'How strange talking is', she writes in a letter to Lady Ottoline Morrell '– what mists rise and fall – how one loses the other & then thinks to have found the other – then down comes another soft final curtain . . . But it is incredible, don't you feel, how mysterious and isolated we each of us are – at the last' (*CLKM* iv. 252). This strangeness of talk, its mists and curtains, its final mystery and the isolation of the individual, is particularly important in those stories that focus on relationships between couples – 'Psychology', 'The Man without a Temperament', 'A Dill Pickle', from *Bliss and Other Stories*, for example, or 'Mr and Mrs Dove' and 'The Stranger', from *The Garden Party and Other Stories*. In each case, the difficulty of communication and the difficulty of relating to another person are expressed through the complications of conversation. The stories centre around the tension between characters' difficulties of expression, on the one hand, and, on the other hand, the precise, expressively exact and exacting prose through which Mansfield constructs in language these scenes of linguistic miscommunication.

'Psychology' is a tale of missed romantic opportunities, of love that fails through non-communication. The narrative concerns the visit by a fashionably 'modern' novelist who plans to write 'very big novels indeed' to the studio of a writer whose plays have an 'exquisite sense of real English Comedy' (*SS* 187). The visit is tense with unspoken desires, with the sense that, if only they could find a way to express it, the two could acknowledge their passion for each other and become lovers. But it ends in failure as they manage to express only superficial and clichéd ideas on topics such as the 'future of the psychological novel'. The story opens with a brief, single-sentence paragraph that both invokes and undercuts a certain emotion by adopting the woman's mannerisms of speech: 'When she opened the door and saw him standing there she was more pleased than ever before, and he, too, as he followed her into the studio, seemed very, very happy to have come' (*SS* 186). There is an expressiveness about this opening that is constituted by a lack of expression: flat, prosaic in its lexical banality, the sentence is also suspiciously and naively enthusiastic in its superlatives and its redundant repetition ('she was more pleased than ever before' and 'very very happy'). The opening is concerned with what Wordsworth calls the 'sad incompetence of human speech'.[3] But, as Wordsworth realized, it is precisely this incompetence, this inexpressiveness, that is expressive, since – in the case of Mansfield's opening – it conveys a powerful sense of superficiality, of naive enthusiasm, of an absence of self-reflection. In a way that Dickens explores in the speech of many of his characters, that Joyce had exploited with a certain narratorial sleight of hand in *Dubliners* and that Samuel Beckett would develop very differently later in the century, Mansfield's opening is expressive in its representation of inexpressiveness, subtle and carefully nuanced in its representation of the crass imperfections of everyday speech. And the sentence suggests something of a 'postmodern' fascination with superficiality, with the way in which social worlds are constructed through surfaces. The risks of such a narrative strategy – a strategy central to Mansfield's development of her technique of impersonation – are, of course, very high. Just as the work of the contemporary American poet John Ashbery constantly verges on banality by its evocation of the banality – the 'sad incompetence' – of human speech patterns, so Mansfield's stories (modernist precursors of the postmodern fascination with surfaces) are constantly in danger of collapsing into the bathos, the melodrama, the sentimentality that constitute their materials.

Complicating this is the fact that in 'Psychology' Mansfield focuses on the discrepancy between what is articulated in conversation and what the characters would like to say. Ironically, despite the fact that both are writers, their conversation is highly inarticulate; similarly, in spite of their declared interest in psychology and in the new science of psychoanalysis, they lack insight into the psychodynamics of their own relationship. As the man enters the woman's studio, the following exchange occurs:

> Their secret selves whispered:
> 'Why should we speak? Isn't this enough?'
> 'More than enough. I never realized until this moment...'
> 'How good it is just to be with you...'
> 'Like this...'
> 'It's more than enough.'
> But suddenly he turned and looked at her and she moved quickly away.
> 'Have a cigarette? I'll put the kettle on. Are you longing for tea?'
> 'No. Not longing.'
> 'Well, I am.'
> 'Oh, you.' He thumped the Armenian cushion and flung on to the *sommier*. 'You're a perfect little Chinee.'
> 'Yes, I am,' she laughed. 'I long for tea as strong men long for wine.'
> (*SS* 186)

The perfect accord of the conversation that takes place – or fails to take place – between the characters' 'secret selves' is indicated by the extent to which their mutual agreement is built around abstraction, generalization, and incomplete sentences. But this unspoken accord contrasts painfully with the triviality and the subtle misfirings of the articulated speech of the couple. Just as when the man turns to look at the woman she moves quickly away, the interchange is constituted by a nervous series of movements towards and anxious movements away. The decadent and self-ironic question 'Are you longing for tea?' is met by an inappropriate seriousness and literalness of response. The

man's violence towards the exotically foreign furniture under-
lines the implications of potential but hidden psychic aggression
in his forcefully informal denomination of her as 'Chinee'. But
the aggression – experienced consciously neither by the man
nor by the woman, we can surmise – is diffused, as the comment
succeeds in reinforcing the woman's sense of her own
interesting exoticism. As the story proceeds, the conversation
becomes increasingly fraught, not least because of the couple's
high expectations of mutual understanding: the possibility
dawns that they are 'just a little too quick, too prompt with
their replies, too ready to take each other up'. The meeting
becomes formulaic, a 'wonderfully good imitation of other
occasions', as the veneer of sociability – of love even – begins to
crack:

> His heart beat; her cheek burned and the stupid thing was she could
> not discover where exactly they were or what exactly was happening.
> She hadn't time to glance back. And just as she had got so far it
> happened again. They faltered, wavered, broke down, were silent.
> Again they were conscious of the boundless, questioning dark.
> Again, there they were – two hunters, bending over their fire, but
> hearing suddenly from the jungle beyond a shake of wind and a
> loud, questioning cry... (SS 189)

As the conversation spins out of control, the metaphors suggest
the lurking danger, the mental violence and terror that will be
the result of the failure of this conversation, a failure that for
these potential lovers, lovers who are no longer in the first blush
of youth ('old enough to enjoy their adventure to the full
without any stupid emotional complication [...] he was thirty-
one, she was thirty' (SS 187)), could be catastrophic, especially
for the woman: their 'precious friendship' threatened, she is in
danger of being 'destroyed' (SS 189). The conversation is, finally,
a deconstruction of conversation, as the couple repeatedly
attempt a gamut of conversational gambits – recently read
novels, psychoanalysis, the state of the modern novel, contemporary society – repeatedly succeeding in conveying to
themselves the sense that real communication is or might be
taking place, but repeatedly overstepping the mark, mistiming
their comments, misjudging tone and intention, above all
revealing the *constructed*, artificial nature of all conversation,
its distance from a kind of idealized notion of communication

beyond language ('Why should we speak? Isn't this enough?') and collapsing back into awkward, non-communicative silence. They become bored with their own conversation, with their own 'heavy, stodgy, elderly' minds (SS 190). The conversation is deconstructive precisely because of the way that it analyses an 'aporia' of conversational desire – the desire to go beyond the conventions of conversation, to speak from the heart with passionate sincerity and the impossibility, precisely because of the desire, to do so.

In each of these stories – in 'Bliss', 'The Voyage', 'Psychology' – as in many others, Mansfield develops, in precisely varied ways, her strategy of indirection and impersonation. In each case, the work involved in the reading – the interpretation – of the story may be said to involve a risky enactment of the subject of the story itself. And in each case, Mansfield insists, in the 'hesitations, doubts, beginnings' of her prose, on the threat of communication collapsing back into the inexpressive, formulaic, or unwitting language of characters whose voices and whose linguistic and mental habits she at the same time so deftly performs.

4

Katherine Mansfield's 'vagrant self'

Katherine Mansfield's identities are bound up with her sense of place and her sense of belonging, national, geographical, cultural, linguistic. But after leaving New Zealand in 1908 Mansfield rarely felt settled and she wrote as a displaced, even, in a certain sense, a homeless person, from a migrant perspective. Hers was what she herself referred to in a letter as a 'vagrant self' (*CLKM* ii. 188). In this chapter we will examine this sense of displacement in Mansfield's writing before going on to discuss the significance of her first home, New Zealand, in and for her writing.

After leaving home and travelling to England for the first time at the age of 14, Mansfield rarely lived in one place for more than a few months at a time, and, despite her efforts to establish a home in England with Murry, for much of her adult life she lived in temporary lodgings, hotels and hostels, guest houses and pensions. Antony Alpers suggests, for example, that at a 'conservative count' Mansfield 'amassed a total of twenty-nine postal addresses' between her arrival in London in 1908 and April 1916 (*L.* 201). The difficulties involved in finding a place to live were no doubt multiple and included the difficulties in her relationship with Murry, her terminal illness, and a chronic lack of money. But the problem also seems to have been to do with a fundamental sense of unease concerning the question of 'home', which we might link with Mansfield's complex and indeed multiple national and cultural identities. From November 1915 until her death, Mansfield repeatedly travelled to the Continent, moving from one temporary residence to another on the French or Italian Riviera, in Paris or Switzerland, in search of a climate that would help to cure her tuberculosis, usually returning to London for the summer. Her condition during these years – the years of her major work – was that of the exile, the migrant, the nomad. Her condition was characterized by the loss of place, by ungrounding or displacement – cultural, geographical, linguistic, national. But from early on in her life Mansfield herself recognized that this loss of place, of permanence, was also a gain in that it allowed for a fluidity or mobility of identity. In a letter to her cousin Sylvia Payne from London in April 1906, Mansfield comments on how much she is enjoying what she calls 'this Hotel life': 'There is a kind of feeling of irresponsibility about it', she says, 'that is fascinating'. And she links this irresponsible life with writing: 'Would you not like to try *all* sorts of lives', she asks her cousin, 'but that is the satisfaction of writing – one can impersonate so many people' (*CLKM* i. 19).

As Roger Robinson has commented, Mansfield's characters are 'ceaselessly on the move, travelling, wandering, often in foreign or threatening situations', and, as he also comments, her stories are filled with 'outcasts, exiles, minorities, and fringe dwellers'.[1] Often in transit, on the move, then, Mansfield's people are often hotel guests or lodgers, people with no fixed abode, on the way to somewhere else. 'The Woman at the Store' focuses on a group of travellers in the unwelcoming, uncanny New Zealand backbush; 'Prelude' concerns the Burnell family's move to a new house in the country; 'Pictures' centres around Ada Moss's attempt to earn enough money to avoid being evicted for non-payment of rent; the characters in 'The Man without a Temperament' live uneasily in a hotel on the Italian Riviera; 'The Little Governess' is concerned with a young woman's difficult, even dangerous journey to Germany; 'Life of Ma Parker' concludes with Ma Parker's distress over the fact that she has no place to be alone to mourn her life; in 'Marriage à la Mode' William is made to feel a stranger in his own house by his wife and her fashionably bohemian friends; 'The Voyage' concerns Fenella's journey by sea to stay with her grandparents after her mother's death; 'The Stranger' revolves around a husband's anxious wait for his wife's ship to dock after her long absence abroad; 'Epilogue I: Pension Seguin' revolves around the narrator's attempt to find lodgings in a strange city. This concern with what is the often disturbing and even threatening nature of travel and with the uncertainties of hotel life is no doubt linked to Mansfield's sense of the insecurities and fragilities of personal identity. But it is also surely impelled, in the first place, by her 'colonial' status, by her move from New Zealand to Europe. As the New Zealand writer and critic C. K. Stead has commented, the cost of Mansfield's 'transplantation' from New Zealand to Europe was 'enormous' and became an important element in her writing, not least in her return to New Zealand as a subject in some of her major stories.[2] But Stead also raises the question of whether Mansfield should be described as a 'New Zealand writer' at all, suggesting that what he calls her 'New Zealandness' is 'hard to pin down' since it has been 'laid over, concealed – deliberately'.[3]

In fact, Mansfield's often somewhat nostalgic desire after her departure in 1908 to return to the place and time of her New Zealand childhood through her writing – 'New Zealand is in my very bones,' she writes in one letter; 'what wouldn't I give to have a look at it' (*LKM* ii. 199) – was no doubt reinforced by the fact that her status in England was that of what she herself called a 'colonial'.[4] Indeed, her notebooks and letters give a powerful sense of the condition of the life of a colonial exile in the metropolitan centre, the condition of being, as Angela Carter puts it, a 'prodigal daughter' in a world 'of which she was subtly never a part'.[5] In one notebook entry, for example, Mansfield remembers – without apparent bitterness – an incident from her time at Queen's College when the Principal referred to her in class as 'a little savage from New Zealand' (*KMN* ii. 31). In another notebook entry Mansfield writes a surreal fantasy of being shouted at by the 'red geraniums' who have bought the garden 'over my head':

> But why should they make me feel a stranger? Why should they ask me every time I go near: 'And what are *you* doing in a London garden?' They burn with arrogance & pride. And I am the little colonial walking in the London garden patch – allowed to look, perhaps, but not to linger. If I lie on the grass they positively shout at me. Look at her lying on *our* grass, pretending she lives here, pretending this is her garden & that tall back of the house with the windows open & the coloured curtains lifting is her house. She is a stranger – an alien. She is nothing but a little girl sitting on the

Tinakori hills & dreaming: I went to London and married an englishman & we lived in a tall grave house with red geraniums & white daisies in the garden at the back. *Im*-pudence! (*KMN* ii. 166)

Mansfield's sense of being a 'stranger', an 'alien', is exacerbated by the unwritten rules that govern one's claim to a place, to a home. Her life in England is only a 'pretence', a dream, even. Mansfield's reaction to such rejection was often extreme. In a notebook, for example, she describes being 'possessed' all day by 'my hate of England', a hatred that is (together with her brief love affair with Francis Carco) her 'one passion – a loathing for England' (*KMN* ii. 5). 'How I have hated England!' she declares later in a letter dated 25 July 1921 from Switzerland: 'Never, never will I live there. It's a kind of negation to me and there is always a kind of silky web or net of complications spread to catch one' (*CLKM* iv. 255). In another notebook, Mansfield's feelings towards her 'typical english husband' are complicated by his 'English' lack of warmth, by the fact that he is not 'ardent, eager, full of quick response, careless, spendthrift of himself, vividly alive, *high spirited*': it is this that she hates in England, a country she never wants to see again: 'No, I don't want England. England is of no use to me' (*KMN* ii. 167).

Mansfield's experience of growing up in New Zealand provided her with a store of memories and, more importantly perhaps, a desire to write herself back to her past and back to her homeland. Her past becomes, indeed, another country. 'Now – now I want to write recollections of my own country', she remarks in a notebook some time after the death of her brother in the First World War, 'not only because it is a "sacred debt" that I pay to my country because my brother & I were born there, but also because in my thoughts I range with him over all the remembered places. I am never far away from them. I long to renew them in writing.' Writing is figured here as a practice that renews the writer's memory, allowing her to re-experience what is lost. As her thoughts on the subject of writing New Zealand develop, she imagines the details of her birthplace:

And the people, the people we loved there. Of them too I want to write – another 'debt of love'. Oh, I want for one moment to make our undiscovered country leap into the eyes of the old world. It must be mysterious, as though floating – it must take the breath [...] I shall tell everything, even of how the laundry basket squeaked at '75'

– but all must be told with a sense of mystery, a radiance, an after glow because you, my little sun of it, are set... (*KMN* ii. 32)

Out of this desire to tell of how the 'laundry basket squeaked at "75" ', Mansfield made some of her most accomplished fictions – 'Prelude', 'At the Bay', 'The Garden Party', 'The Doll's House', and others. But as well as being important 'New Zealand' stories, the ethnic, national, and cultural identifications of many of these narratives are complicated by the way that the class and cultural assumptions of characters' thoughts and actions are overlaid by an 'English' sensibility. As Stead remarks, Mansfield 'neutraliz[es] the background' in many of these stories.[6] In other words, the Burnell and the Sheridan stories may themselves be read as articulations of the placelessness, or perhaps more accurately the multiple placings, the multiple cultural, ethnic, and national identifications of Mansfield's identity.

In a number of earlier stories, however – 'The Woman at the Store', 'Ole Underwood', and 'Millie' – Mansfield evokes a colonial cultural identity that is peculiarly un-English, an identity, indeed, constituted by its difference from the English. Although the stories have had a somewhat marginal place in the Mansfield canon, Stead has stressed their importance in a number of essays written since the 1970s and two of them have found a place in Angela Smith's new edition of the Oxford World's Classics *Selected Stories*. In these three stories, Mansfield develops themes and a style that, according to Stead 'indicate a whole line of development she denied herself by becoming a European writer' (*CR* 158) – a line of development that is particularly influential in the work of other New Zealand writers of the 1930s–1950s.[7] The three stories may be read both as important literary 'roads not taken' in Mansfield's career and as in themselves interesting and not unproblematic considerations of cultural and national identity. As I will suggest, the stories demonstrate that Mansfield's cultural and national identity as a 'New Zealander' is itself no less complicated than her sense of cultural identity as a 'colonial' in England and Europe.

First published by Murry in *Rhythm* and *The Blue Review* in 1912 and 1913, 'The Woman at the Store', 'Ole Underwood', and 'Millie' were begun not long after Mansfield left New Zealand but written in what Antony Alpers characterizes as a state of 'cultural isolation that was total': 'no one who read them in

London', comments Alpers, 'could have known what in fact they achieved' (*L.* 155). It is intriguing to contemplate Alpers's sense that Mansfield is not only a displaced person but a displaced author, an author at this point, and in these stories at least, without an audience, living what she termed, in her early fantasy of such a life, a 'dual existence' (*KMN* i. 111). Alpers suggests that Mansfield's cultural and geographical displacement means that her audience – the literary and avant-garde community of London in particular – is, in a certain sense, culturally illiterate with regard to the locations and language of her writing, that her stories have no proper, no properly educated readers. Indeed, Angela Smith remarks that 'The Woman at the Store' is 'disorientating' for the reader, 'inverting' as it does the 'conventions of European writing' (larks are cacophonous, sunset is sudden and 'grotesque', and so on): 'Nothing is what is seems,' Smith comments, and suggests that the reader feels that she is being 'sneered at'.[8] Mansfield is, of course, well aware of the problem of the possible alienation of her readers from her New Zealand stories. Writing to Murry about the contents of *Bliss and Other Stories* in February 1920, she says that she couldn't have 'The Woman at the Store' reprinted in the volume (*CLKM* iii. 210). And she hints at a reason for this refusal in a review of her compatriot, Jane Mander's, novel *The Story of a New Zealand River* in July of the same year. Her comments seem to confirm Alpers's sense that New Zealand writing is, at some level, unreadable for an English audience. 'In spite of the fact that there is frequent allusion to the magnificent scenery,' she remarks of Mander's novel, 'it profiteth us nothing', since references to indigenous New Zealand plants with alien, Maori names – the 'laurel-like puriris', the 'lacy rimu', the 'hard blackish kahikateas', and the 'oak-like ti-tokis' – can mean little to the English reader. 'What picture can that possibly convey to an English reader?', she asks, 'What emotion can it produce?'[9]

All three of Mansfield's early New Zealand stories centre around violence and lawlessness – indeed, all three centre on an act of murder: 'The Woman at the Store' concerns a woman living in the isolation of the New Zealand backblocks who, her daughter indicates, has murdered her husband; 'Ole Underwood' centres on the eponymous protagonist's murder of his unfaithful wife and ends in the suggestion that he will kill again; 'Millie' tells of the murder of Mr Williamson by his English apprentice farmhand and the blood-lust of those that are hunting him down in order to take their own revenge. These bleak, violent narratives are played out against a raw and unforgiving landscape. Although Mansfield wrote about murder and violence in other stories – indeed, violence is, I will suggest, an ever-present dimension in many of her fictions – in her later work violence is often qualified by (if not constituted as) the decorum of English and European society. In 'The Woman at the Store', 'Ole Underwood', and 'Millie', however, Mansfield seems to suggest that New Zealand society is constituted precisely in its absence, an absence of cultural and social conventions that allows undisguised physical violence – usually unpunished or at least not punished by official legal process and in that sense too outside the law – to predominate.

'The Woman at the Store' is told by one of three travellers in the New Zealand backblocks. The three come near to an isolated store that one of them, Hin, has previously visited. Hin tells his fellow travellers that the store is owned by a man who will 'give yer a bottle of whisky before 'e shakes hands with yer' and his wife who will 'promise you something else before she shakes hands with you' (SS 10–11). As they arrive at the store, they find the woman alone with her daughter. The woman tells the travellers that her husband is 'away shearin'' (SS 12). She is a disappointment to the travellers, though, for, despite Hin's boast that she is famous for knowing one hundred and twenty-five different ways of kissing (SS 14), she is decidedly unattractive: 'you felt there was nothing but sticks and wires under that pinafore – her front teeth were knocked out, she had red pulpy hands, and she wore on her feet a pair of dirty "Bluchers"' (SS 12). Jo, however, is philosophical, telling Hin that 'she'll look better by night light' and that, anyway, 'she's female flesh!' (SS 14). The woman tells the travellers that she has had four miscarriages since her marriage six years ago and that if they were 'back at the Coast' she would have had her husband 'lynched for child murder': 'Over and over I tells 'im – you've broken my spirit and spoiled my looks', she says (SS 16). 'Trouble with me is', she goes on, 'he left me too much alone' (SS 16), perhaps confirming Hin and the narrator's suspicion that the isolation has made her 'mad' (SS 13). After a night in which the woman's daughter – a 'mean, undersized brat, with whitish hair, and weak eyes' (*SS* 15) – draws a picture of 'the woman shooting at a man with a rook rifle and then digging a hole to bury him in' (*SS* 19), Hin and the narrator leave, while Jo, who has apparently tried out some of the woman's 'one hundred and twenty-five ways' of kissing over night, calls ominously to tell them that he'll catch up with them later. Ole Underwood, in the story of the same name, is also, apparently 'cracked' (*SKM* 132). Tormented by a thudding noise, the noise of something beating in his breast 'like a hammer' (*SKM* 131), Ole Underwood makes his way into a town (based on Wellington, although it remains unnamed) and into a pub where he is studiously avoided. One of the customers tells another Ole Underwood's story: 'When he was a young fellow, thirty years ago, a man 'ere done in 'is woman, an' 'e foun' out an' killed 'er' – for which he was given twenty years in jail and ended up 'cracked'. The storyteller does not know who 'did in' Underwood's wife: 'Dunno', he says, ' 'E don' no, nor nobody' (*SKM* 132). Overhearing the story, Ole Underwood crushes some 'red pinks' that stand in a jar on the counter and is hounded from the bar. Hounded again even from another group of outsiders – a group of Chinese men playing cards – he eventually makes his way to the wharf, which, as an ex-sailor, he remembers well, and into the cabin of a ship. In the cabin a sailor is asleep on a bunk and, to Underwood's crazed imagination, there is a picture of his dead wife above the sailor, 'her picture – his woman's picture – smiling and smiling at the big sleeping man' (*SKM* 133). The story ends here, but with the suggestion that Underwood will, despite the bar customer's assurance that ' 'E's 'armless enough' (*SKM* 132), murder the sleeping – and presumably innocent – man. 'Millie' is told from the perspective of Millie Evans, who is alone on a farm while her husband, Sid, helps hunt for Harrison, a 'young English "johnny" ' who has disappeared after the shooting of Mr Williamson. 'My word! When they caught that young man!' Millie thinks: 'As Sid said, if he wasn't strung up where would they all be?' (*SS* 24). But when Millie comes across a young man hiding near the house and recognizes Harrison, instead of revealing him, she feeds him and helps him hide. 'Nothing but a kid', she thinks, 'An' all them fellows after 'im. 'E don't stand any more of a chance than a kid would [...] They won't ketch 'im. Not if I can 'elp it. Men is all beasts. I don't care wot 'e's done, or wot 'e 'asn't done. See 'im through, Millie Evans,' she tells herself (SS 27). The scene changes to the night with Sid and his mates back on the farm. As Harrison tries to escape under cover of darkness, he is discovered and the men run after him. Despite her sense that the 'justice' that the men have been talking about is 'all [...] rot', and that you don't 'know what anythink's like till yer do know' (SS 27–8), as the men chase after Harrison, Millie's mood changes. She feels 'a strange mad joy' that 'smother[s] everything else' and she laughs, shrieks, and dances, shouting for the men to catch Harrison, to 'Shoot 'im down. Shoot 'im!' (SS 28).

The three early stories, then, are uncompromisingly 'colonial' in their New Zealand setting and language, and impelled by relatively straightforward narrative trajectories: each is plotted around a killing that takes place either outside the law, outside society, or within the context of a crude and crudely reasoned logic of retributive justice. And yet the stories are, perhaps, more complicated in their analysis of ethnic and national identity than this sense of a desocialized New Zealand naturalism might suggest, just as the 'naturalism' of Mansfield's prose is itself complicated by devices of parallelism, indirection, and symbolism. While New Zealand is presented as a place of lawlessness and outlawry, a place of the outsider, the stories complicate this sense of a New Zeland 'identity' by suggesting its involvement in a context of British imperialism. While many of Mansfield's later New Zealand stories – 'The Garden Party', 'The Dolls House', 'How Pearl Button was Kidnapped', and others – suggest that a powerful dimension of New Zealand society is as a simulacrum of England, in 'The Woman at the Store', 'Ole Underwood', and 'Millie', the imperial power is represented as an uncanny presence within the otherness of New Zealand settler culture. The three stories are unflinchingly and uncompromisingly brutal in their representation of settler life, but in two of the three stories Mansfield also focuses briefly on the connections and discontinuities of the brutal, working-class New Zealand culture to that of the British colonial power, to an alienated Englishness. In both cases, England becomes the anachronistic and dislocated background – indeed, literally the faded wallpaper – for New Zealand life. In 'The Woman at the

Store' the unnamed woman of the title lives in a house that is an incongruous mix of backblock poverty – almost destitution – and the faded remnants of English gentility:

> It was a large room, the walls plastered with old pages of English periodicals. Queen Victoria's Jubilee appeared to be the most recent number – a table with an ironing board and wash-tub on it – some wooden forms – a black horsehair sofa, and some broken cane chairs pushed against the walls. The mantlepiece above the stove was draped in pink paper, further ornamented with dried grasses and ferns and a coloured print of Richard Seddon. (*SS* 12)

The symbolism of colonial power, represented not least in its head of state, has been cannibalized and transformed into wallpaper – England *is*, in a sense, the forgotten wallpaper in this scene, overlaid by an alternative governance in the picture of Richard Seddon, the prime minister of New Zealand until 1906. The contrasting savagery of New Zealand is explicitly evoked in the next paragraph: 'There is no twilight to our New Zealand days, but a curious half-hour when everything appears grotesque – it frightens – as though the savage spirit of the country walked abroad and sneered at what it saw' (*SS* 13). While New Zealand – New Zealandness – is, on the one hand, brutal, grotesque, terrifying, this seems to suggest, it is, on the other hand, constituted by an incongruous and anachronistic royalism – one that, however, has been cannibalized and distorted in its transportation to the New Zealand backblocks.

A similar evocation of cultural dislocation is also apparent in 'Millie', which once again marks such a difference by the incongruity of the furnishings and fittings of the New Zealand domestic interior:

> She flopped down on the side of the bed and stared at the coloured print on the wall opposite, 'Garden Party at Windsor Castle'. In the foreground emerald lawns planted with immense oak trees, and in their grateful shade, a muddle of ladies and gentlemen and parasols and little tables. The background was filled with the towers of Windsor Castle, flying three Union Jacks, and in the middle of the picture the old Queen, like a tea cosy with a head on top of it. 'I wonder if it really looked like that.' Millie stared at the flowery ladies, who simpered back at her. 'I wouldn't care for that sort of thing. Too much side. What with the Queen an' one thing an' another'. (*SS* 25)

41

The Englishness of the print is marked as both overbearing and anachronistic by the image of the three Union Jacks and by the presence of Queen Victoria. And it is contrasted immediately with Millie's contemplation of another scene, specifically of New Zealand but equally fabricated and artificial: she turns from the coloured print to look at a photograph of her wedding, where she and her husband pose in front of 'some fern trees, and a waterfall, and Mount Cook in the distance, covered with snow' (SS 25). But the image of colonial power is deeply ironized and its potency as ideology compromised by the very rhetoric of the description. By contrast with the Windsor Castle scene – with its sophistication (including the alienating 'side'), its symbolic complexity (or in Millie's terms 'muddle'), and its aristocratic context (suggested by the 'emerald' lawn, by the gentlemen and ladies, and even by the parasols) – Millie's language is direct and even crude: her language is syntactically repetitive ('and ... and ... and ... and') and she perhaps unwittingly undermines the head of state's dignity by her crass figuration of the Queen as a tea cosy with a head on top. Millie's doubt over whether the tea party at Windsor castle 'really looked like that' is, indeed, a central question in a story involving the murder of a New Zealander by an Englishman. The transplantation of English culture into a New Zealand context leads to the question of what that culture 'really' looks like. In other words, Mansfield suggests that the representational *power* of imperial Britain – the power, that is, to represent – is compromised in its migration to a different hemisphere. The transplantation or transportation of 'English' representational conventions to those of New Zealand settler culture leads not only to a distortion of its pictures of itself, but also to an undermining of the very representational conventions by which empire constitutes itself.

These New Zealand stories, then, with their tales of violence, their setting of economic and cultural deprivation, their raw, colloquial speech patterns, and their harsh, unsentimental idioms, articulate a raw energy of national and cultural origin rarely found elsewhere in Mansfield's work. But the intrusion of Britishness into the cultural background in two of the stories evinces a heightened awareness of the complexity of a New Zealand cultural identity. One of the identities that Mansfield takes on or performs is that of the 'colonial', of the 'little savage from New Zealand'. In other stories this identification is submerged within a different kind of class allegiance and a different kind of cosmopolitanism. But New Zealand – as identity and identification – is a place that defines Mansfield, above all, as displaced, as placeless. Cultural and national identity, we might surmise, was, for Mansfield, another aspect of the complex representation of personal identity and impersonality that we are calling 'impersonation'.

5

'A queer state':
Writing Gender and Sexuality

As we have seen, the question of Mansfield's impersonations is not just a literary question and is not restricted to her fictions. Impersonation was important in Mansfield's life as well as being critical to her writing: impersonation for Mansfield was partly a condition of being a writer and partly a condition of being. On at least one occasion in her letters and notebooks – a rich source of speculation on writing and on the nature of the writer's work – Mansfield represents the 'double life' of the writer as what she calls a 'queer state', queer because of the way that the writer is detached from life, depersonalized. 'I feel in my heart as though I have died – as far as personal life goes,' she writes to Dorothy Brett in December 1918: 'I am a writer who cares for nothing but writing – thats how I feel. When I am with people I feel like a doctor with his patients – very sympathetic [...] but as regards myself – quite alone – quite isolated – a queer state' (*CLKM* ii. 296).[1] The problem of this double life, of the detachment of the writer from her own life, is also a problem, not least, of gender. In two letters written in 1919, Mansfield tried to explain to Murry her sense of the splitting-apart of the writer and the woman. 'I live *withdrawn* from my personal life', she remarks in a letter dated 12 December: 'I am a writer first.' And she contrasts her present state with that of the past, when she worked less and when 'my writing self was merged in my personal self' (*CLKM* iv. 149). A few days earlier, on 3 December 1919, Mansfield had linked this sense of authorship with her relationship with Murry and more generally with the question of gender and sexuality. She tells Murry that she is unable to 'give' him '*all*' that he wants: 'Im a writer first & a woman after', she says (*CLKM* iv. 133).[2] The comment highlights a central problem in Mansfield's writing and in her life, its 'queer state', one that she struggled with throughout her life and that she never reconciled. It is a problem that involves the queerness not just of her relationship with Murry but of her sense of herself as a writer and the complex interactions between writing, gender, and sexuality. The poetics of impersonation – the sense that Mansfield's fictions are constructed around the withdrawal of authorial personhood and the adoption of other voices, other modes of being – is as relevant to Mansfield's sense of gender and sexuality as it is to other aspects of her life and work. As Mary Burgan argues, the 'anxious dialectic of the erotic' in Mansfield's early adult life generated a 'plethora of roles to play, costumes to assume and evasions to perform as she defined herself sexually'.[3] Mansfield's complaint against Murry is, of course, a complaint against his patriarchal assumption that she adopts the 'domestic' role appropriate to a stereotyped femininity. But she is also suggesting that the condition of writing – the condition by which it can occur – involves the suspension or questioning of the conventions of gender and sexual identification. In this chapter, I will suggest that gender and sexuality are complex, conflicted questions in Mansfield's writing, that gender and sexuality in her fictions are, in more than one sense, 'queer'.

In recent years, critics have re-evaluated Mansfield as a writer who has both a specifically feminine, and a specifically feminist, language, role, and perspective. As they have suggested, the letters and journals give a vivid sense of a young woman coming to maturity at a time when *fin de siècle* gender definitions were being redefined and sexual roles reinvented. One of the roles that Mansfield adopted in her early adulthood was what came to be known later in the twentieth century as 'queer'. Fascinated by Wilde, whose literary aestheticism also carried with it a certain sexual 'dissidence', Mansfield experimented in her youth with both the perverse contradictoriness of a Wildean aphoristic style and homosexual – in her case lesbian – desire. In her late teens and early twenties Mansfield had a number of female lovers and even pondered at one point whether the 'kernel of the whole matter' of herself might be what she called 'the Oscar-like thread' of her passions (*KMN* i. 103). In fact, as Sydney

Kaplan has argued, the influence of Oscar Wilde – to Mansfield a 'model and terror' – continued throughout her life as an 'impetus toward the idolization of art as a means of *controlling* the forbidden while allowing it, nonetheless, oblique expression'.[4] But Mansfield also 'experimented' as a young woman with other modes of desire and other gender identifications, including heterosexuality, masochistic passion, and masculinity, and more generally with a sexual and emotional freedom unusual for her time.

Mansfield's early interest in issues of gender and sexuality included an interest in the emancipation of women and at times an identification of herself with what might anachronistically be called 'feminism'. Indeed, critics such as Sydney Kaplan and Kate Fullbrook have suggested that Mansfield may be defined as a 'feminist' writer. Kaplan argues that, whatever 'definition for her own awareness she might have chosen', Mansfield's life and writing are characterized by 'an emerging feminist consciousness',[5] and, attempting to overcome the problem that Mansfield's feminism is largely invisible, Fullbrook argues that her 'feminism came as a matter of course, so much so that overt discussion of it as a political principle is absent from her writing while its underlying presence is everywhere'.[6] But I want to suggest that (as both Kaplan and Fullbrook in fact recognize) 'feminism' is often rather more difficult and more troubling for Mansfield than these comments might indicate, that definitions of both feminism and femininity are constantly in process, constantly under negotiation, constantly being constructed and subverted in her work. On a number of occasions in the early notebooks and letters Mansfield certainly expresses an unequivocally feminist perspective:

> I feel that I do now realise, dimly, what women in the future will be capable of achieving. They truly, as yet, have never had their chance. Talk of our enlightened days and our emancipated country – pure nonsense. We are firmly held in the self fashioned chains of slavery. Yes – now I see that they are self fashioned and must be self removed.   (*KMN* i. 110)

The interest here is not only in the young Mansfield's early identification with women's emancipation (she is referring to the fact that women in New Zealand gained the vote as early as

1893) but also in her sense that the 'liberation' of women has to do with an escape from their 'self fashioning'. This notebook entry was written after reading the American actress Elizabeth Robins's feminist novel *Come and Find Me* (1908), and for some time after reading the book Mansfield enthusiastically writes about the liberation of women: in one letter, for example, she comments that she likes to think of Robins as 'only the first of a great never ending procession of splendid, strong woman writers' and that the 'suffragist movement is *excellent* for our sex – kicked policemen or no kicked policemen' (*CLKM* i. 47). And yet these early enthusiasms for the emancipation of women and for the suffragette movement are rarely reflected in her stories. Indeed, the stories are more likely to satirize or ironize enthusiasm for the suffragettes than to indicate support.[7] In 'Being a Truthful Adventure', a story written in 1911, for example, the narrator, Katherine, seems to consider enthusiasm for female suffrage to be part of a past that she has left behind on travelling to Europe. The story centres around Katherine's experience of a visit to Bruges and her sense of detachment both from the locals and from the tourists that she meets. The story ends in a chance meeting with Betty, a friend from school in New Zealand, and her husband, both of whom immediately declare themselves to be 'frightfully keen on the Suffrage' (*SKM* 101): 'I always had the idea you were so frightfully keen on the future of women,' remarks Betty to Katherine (*SKM* 101–2). The story – 'truthful' or not with respect to Mansfield's own experiences during her visit to Bruges in 1911 – suggests that the couple's evangelistic passion for female suffrage involves something that 'Katherine' can no longer share.

Feminism also plays a central but satirized part in Mansfield's later story 'A Cup of Tea', published by Murry in the posthumous collection *The Doves' Nest and Other Stories*. 'A Cup of Tea' centres on a rich, fashionable, vain, 'not exactly beautiful' and ultimately frivolous woman, Rosemary Fell, who decides that it will be fun to help save a 'girl' that she comes across begging on the London streets – 'a little battered creature with enormous eyes, someone quite young, no older than herself'. (*SS* 362, 364). Rosemary's is a world in which female solidarity has as much substance as fairy godmothers: 'She was going to prove to this girl that – wonderful things did happen in life, that – fairy godmothers were real, that – rich people had hearts, and that women *were* sisters', and turning to the woman she assures her that she is in safe hands since, as she declares, 'We're both women' (*SS* 365). Rosemary's game of sisterly solidarity, however, quickly evaporates when her husband comments that the 'girl' is 'astonishingly pretty [...] absolutely lovely' (*SS* 368), whereupon the 'not exactly beautiful' Rosemary gives the girl £3, lets her leave the house, and reassures herself of her husband's affection by persuading him to buy her a little enamel antique box costing twenty-eight guineas. The location of 'feminism' in such a story is not at all straightforward, since on one level at least it is the object of satirical attack. Indeed, the story could easily be read as anti-female – femininity here being characterized in terms of the stereotypes of frivolity, vanity, political naivety, inconsistency, and shopping excess – as well as anti-feminist – the attempt at 'feminist' solidarity being easily undermined by patriarchal disapproval. While it is true that, as Kaplan argues, what 'might seem like antifeminism' in Mansfield's work – 'negative portrayals or criticism of women's behavior' – can in fact be read in terms of her 'frustration and anger over many women's refusal to overcome their conditioned acceptance of women's role',[8] in this story a certain 'feminist' solidarity is the central target of Mansfield's irony: Rosemary's 'feminism' is, indeed, a fairy story. To argue, with Fullbrook, that Mansfield's 'feminism' is a 'matter of course' is, in fact, to overlook the tonal and structural complications – the impersonations, indeed – of such a story and to overlook, more generally, the extent to which, for Mansfield, both femininity (and masculinity) and feminism are unstable, conflicted questions, questions indeed that *resist* definition, that are in process, performed, aspects of impersonation.[9]

While Mansfield's youthful enthusiasm for the emancipation of women – qualified and ironized as it is – is rarely expressed in later notebooks and letters, her representation of the complex and often difficult interactions between the sexes as well as the position of women in both New Zealand and European societies of the early twentieth century is acute. As with other aspects of her writing, her analysis of gender and sexuality is rarely straightforward and is always mediated by impersonation. But it is difficult either to dismiss or to celebrate Mansfield as a 'woman' (or a 'women's') writer since her 'position' on such issues is as complex and indeed unsettling as are her identifications and identities in other respects. There is no question, however, that gender – gender identifications, gender impersonations, gender relations as well as sexual desires, relations, and identifications – play an important part in many of Mansfield's stories. And in many cases a critique of patriarchal structures and attitudes with their attendant oppression of women is an important element in the stories. In both 'Prelude' and 'At the Bay', for example, the underlying antagonism between women and men and the sense that women are pressurized by men – under constant pressure to 'be' feminine, including sexually 'feminine' – is expressed by the relief that women feel when Stanley leaves the family home to go to work. In 'Prelude', Linda cannot rest until 'the final slam of the front door' assures her that 'Stanley was really gone' (*SS* 92), after which the whole household seems to experience relief. The relief is even more palpable in the repetition of Stanley's departure in 'At the Bay'. Here the effect is likened to an 'infection' amongst the women: 'Oh, the relief, the difference it made to have the man out of the house. Their very voices were changed as they called to one another; they sounded warm and loving and as if they shared a secret' (287). And this motif of release from the male presence is reconfirmed when the widow Mrs Stubbs tells Alice, to the latter's dismay, that, despite her husband's 'fine face', 'freedom's best!' (303). The motif is also expressed in an earlier 'Burnell' story from 1912, 'The Little Girl', in which Kezia experiences a 'glad sense of relief' on the departure of her father (*SKM* 120). This sense of relief is no doubt related to the economic and social dependence of women on men in the society depicted in the stories: as Kaplan suggests, the 'vulnerability of women when they must depend on men for economic and emotional support is a continuing theme in Mansfield's writing'.[10] But in Mansfield this 'theme' results, more often than not, in the satirizing of women themselves, in an ironizing of women's socialized dependence on men alongside her critique of the pressures that women place on other women to conform to a certain model of femininity. Often oblique, subtly challenging the reader to construct her own sense of the oppressions of female society itself, Mansfield's critique is indirectly stated, or understated, performed rather or played out by her characters. In her unfinished story 'The Doves' Nest', for example, Miss Anderson's frustration at the limitations of 'feminine' company leads her to suggest that 'ladies by themselves are [...] apt to find their interests limited' owing to the 'absence of political discussion' (*SKM* 520). But Milly's answer both misses Miss Anderson's point and at the same time confirms it: '"Oh, politics!" cried Milly, airily. "I hate politics. Father always said — "' (*SKM* 520).

Femininity – femininity as bound up in heterosexual desire and desirability – is also represented in Mansfield's stories as a performance, as impersonation. Indeed, the question of femininity, of femaleness, goes to the heart of the problem of Mansfield's engagement with feminism. As Ruth Parkin-Gounelas has suggested, we can read Mansfield as herself 'the most ruthless critic of her own collusion with femininity' and her writing as a 'brilliant enactment but also deconstruction of the feminine code of practice'.[11] Femininity as much as masculinity, indeed, is never a given, never 'natural', but rather learned, enacted, its models and stereotypes acted upon. An exemplary figure for Mansfield's exploration of the constructions – the constructedness – of a certain 'feminine' ideal is Linda's younger sister Beryl in 'Prelude' and 'At the Bay'. In 'Prelude' Beryl is torn between her desire to be desirable – 'fascinating', 'lovely' – and her sense that her fascination with her fascinating, lovely self is 'false' (*SS* 118–19). Standing at her bedroom mirror, Beryl approves of her feminine image: she notes the signifiers of virginity (whiteness) and youth (slimness) by which she constructs and evaluates her own femininity: she sees 'a slim girl in white – a white serge skirt, a white silk blouse, and a leather belt drawn in very tightly at her tiny waist' (*SS* 118). She carefully examines her 'heart-shaped' face, her mouth and 'fascinating' protuding underlip, her nose and her 'Lovely, lovely hair' (*SS* 119). But catching herself admiring herself, she reacts in self-disgust: she is 'false', 'silly and spiteful and vain' (*SS* 119), just 'acting a part': 'Hadn't she put her hand over [Stanley's], pointing out something so that he should see how white her hand was beside his brown one' (*SS* 119). At this point, Beryl is distracted from her search for a troubling authenticity and returns to her 'feminine' – frivolous, flirtatious, socially agreeable role. The story suggests an uneasy self-consciousness with regard to Beryl's sense of her own femininity as well as more generally with regard to Mansfield's concern with and representation of gender difference. There is a paradox here – a paradox of impersonation, we might say – concerning the way in which gender is always for Mansfield an impersonation of gender, a mask, or what the psychoanalyst Joan Riviere – a contemporary of Mansfield – calls the 'masquerade' of femininity.[12] The paradox involves the way that, while femininity is enacted, is a masquerade or performance, to 'catch' oneself acting the part is to experience a disabling self-consciousness about the role, a self-consciousness that produces both a certain self-disgust and a collapse of the performance. And yet the protection against such a troubling recognition involves the (re-)adoption of the role or performance: the protection from self-disgust is the adoption of the very role against which one revolts.

The gender and the sexuality of Mansfield's characters, however, are often not even as clear-cut as this, since both are often indeterminate, qualified, compromised, or complicated. Rather than stable, fixed, permanent, or an aspect of one's 'essential' being, gender is often detached from biological sex in the sense that femininity and masculinity are not necessarily restricted to women and men respectively. In this respect, too, Mansfield's fictions explore the 'masquerade' or impersonation of gender rather than simply producing a critique of predetermined gender roles and conflicts.[13] Gender and sexual identifications that are mobile or insecure are often the focus of Mansfield's stories, and a number of her most compelling creations are characters whose indeterminate or compromised gender and sexual identifications make them troubling or disturbing to others. Duquette, the narrator in 'Je ne parle pas français', for example, is oddly androgynous, although he likes to think of himself as highly attractive to women. His description of himself fuses gender and sexuality but diffuses gender and biological sex. The description of himself is, as Pamela Dunbar puts it, 'laced with indications of femininity'.[14] He is 'little and light' and has 'black eyes with long lashes', 'black silky hair cut short', 'supple and small' hands. Undressed, he tells us, he is 'rather charming': 'Plump, almost like a girl, with smooth shoulders [...] I wear a thin gold bracelet above my left elbow' (*SS* 148). In 'At the Bay', Mrs Harry Kember is heavily masculinized: she is known only by the name of her husband, she lacks 'vanity', speaks to the men 'as though she was one of them', cares little about her house, and is described as 'like a horrible caricature of her husband' (*SS* 292, 294). Rather differently, but also somewhat disturbingly, the narrator of 'The Woman at the Store' has an ambiguous gender identity. The story is narrated by a woman who is travelling with two men but whose gender is veiled except in one brief sentence in which she is referred to as 'she' by a child. Referring to the narrator bathing naked in the creek, the 'kid' remarks that 'I looked at her where she wouldn't see me from' (*SS* 15), a comment that jolts the reader into the recognition that the narrator, who has up to this point been coded as masculine, is in fact a woman. In the rather sentimental story 'Mr and Mrs Dove' Mansfield plays on a reversal of gender roles, on a reversal of stereotypes of masculine dominance and female subservience. In this story, Anne is unable to marry Reggie because she cannot help laughing at him – the 'queer thing' being that 'she didn't herself know why she laughed' (*SS* 260). The laughter – the fact that Anne cannot help laughing at her suitor – de-masculinizes and de-sexualizes Reggie: the man she will marry must accord with the theatrical representations of the masculine lover that she knows so well, must be 'a tall, handsome, brilliant stranger', the kind of man who 'without a word catch[es] the heroine in his arms, and after one long, tremendous look, carr[ies] her off to anywhere' (263). And yet, as the story ends, Anne seems to settle for her emasculated man, calling him back to her, once again. Finally, Mansfield's mixing up of gender and her sense that gender identity is structured by impersonation, by performance, may also be seen to be played out in the different narratorial perspectives, the different narrative voices, that she adopts or performs. She often impersonates male narrators or presents her narratives from the masculine perspective. Stories such as 'Je ne parle pas français', 'The Young Girl', and 'A Married Man's Story' are told by male narrators; while, rather differently, stories such as 'Mr Reginald Peacock's Day', 'Marriage à la mode', 'The Stranger', 'An Ideal Family', and sections of 'Prelude' and 'At the Bay' are told in the third person but with sympathy for and identification with the language and perspective of male characters.

Rather than 'feminist' in any straightforward sense, then, we might more accurately see Mansfield as a writer for whom sexuality and gender are difficult and often troubling issues. Mansfield's stories explore human sexuality in varied but often conflicting ways, Woolf's shocked sense that her fellow writer had 'knocked about with prostitutes'[15] no doubt accounting for her fellow writer's lack of idealism and sentimentality with respect to such relationships. More often than not, in fact, sexuality is represented in Mansfield's stories as an aspect of exploitation, abuse, or manipulation, or as matter of financial exchange. As Dunbar comments, Mansfield challenged many of the myths of her time and dealt in 'dangerous or taboo subjects', including 'child abuse and neglect, prostitution and procuration, murder within marriage, wife-beating, sexual deviation, child sexuality'.[16] In 'Je ne parle pas français', for example, the 10-year-old Raoul Duquette is given fried cakes covered in sugar by an African laundress in exchange for kisses and for allowing her to 'open her bodice and put me to her', making him 'very languid, very caressing, and greedy beyond measure' (SS 147) and accounting for his willingness as an adult to obtain 'right-down cash' in exchange for his sexual favours (SS 148). 'Pictures' ends with Miss Moss, about to be evicted from her lodgings for non-payment of rent and desperate for money, nervously going to the Café de Madrid – telling herself that it is 'a place for artists too' and that as a 'respectable woman' there is no reason why she should not go in – hoping that with a 'stroke of luck' she will find employment as a contralto. She settles instead for the 'stout gentleman' who buys her drinks, and tells her, frankly, that he likes ''em firm and well covered', before the couple leave to spend the night together (SS 199–200). 'The Little Governess' concerns a young English woman on her first trip abroad who encounters a series of threatening situations. She is sexually harassed by a group of young men on the train, not least by their laughter – and by their singing, which gives her a 'queer little tremble in her stomach' (SS 50); the porter punishes her for her paltry tip by allowing a man into her woman-only compartment; and after she fails to tip the waiter at the hotel he is both insolent and sexually insinuating. Befriended by the man in her train compartment who is old enough to be her grandfather and who she fondly thinks of as sexually unthreatening, she ends up almost being raped. With his knee 'twitching against hers' the old man presses her, literally, for a kiss: 'he held her against the wall, pressed against her his hard old body and his twitching knee and, though she shook her head from side to side, distracted, kissed her on the mouth' (SS 58). Beryl Fairfield in the 'Burnell' stories is also repeatedly figured as subject to what might now be called sexual harassment. As her dreams of a lover and a husband at the end of 'At the Bay' merge into the reality of Harry Kember's nocturnal visit, the lovely idea of romance comes up against the 'horror' of his insistent persuasion: 'quick as a cat Harry Kember [...] snatched her to him' (SS 314). As Beryl resists, he calls her a 'Cold little devil' in his 'hateful voice' and her dream of romantic love turns into the 'vile' reality of Kember's angry, urgent sexual demands (SS 314). Beryl appears again in 'The Doll's House', where her dreams of romance are once again undercut by the reality of a relationship with a threatening man: 'The afternoon had been awful. A letter had come from Willie Brent, a terrifying, threatening letter, saying if she did not meet him that evening in Pulman's Bush, he'd come to the front door and ask the reason why!' (SS 356).

As some of these examples suggest, an enduring feature of Mansfield's writing is her analysis of the way that both psychological and physical violence – violent, forced sexuality, in particular – underlie relationships between men and women. The figuration of psychological pain as a kind of violence experienced by rejected lovers or by the unloved is one aspect of Mansfield's representation of sexual relations. 'The Singing Lesson', for example, opens with Miss Meadows feeling 'despair – cold, sharp despair – buried deep in her heart like a wicked knife' after her fiancé has broken off their engagement (SKM 359). Rather differently, in 'Miss Brill' a courting couple's mockery of Miss Brill's clothes and the young man's question – 'who wants her?' (SS 228) – destroy her momentary and fragile sense of happiness. But real, physical violence is also important in Mansfield's stories and in her depiction of sexual relation-ships. The potential and actual physical violence of men towards women is most strikingly apparent in Mansfield's first collec-tion, In a German Pension. 'Frau Brechenmacher Attends a

Wedding', for example, ends with Frau Brechenmacher waiting patiently, passively, for her drunken husband to come to bed: 'She lay down on the bed and put her arm across her face like a child who expected to be hurt as Herr Brechenmacher lurched in' (*SS* 9). 'At "Lehman's"' focuses on the experience of a naive and sexually ignorant cafe waitress, Sabina, who is approached by a more worldly customer. Sabina is sexually aroused without really knowing it: 'Very languid felt Sabina in the hot room, and the Young Man's voice was strong and deep. She thought she had never seen anybody who looked so strong [...] and his restless gaze wandering over her face and figure gave her a curious thrill deep in her body, half pleasure, half pain...(*SKM* 39). But Sabina's ideas about sex are confusingly mixed up with giving birth and with the labour of Frau Lehman. In this story, as in a number of others (notably 'Prelude' and 'At the Bay'), Mansfield conflates ambivalence towards female sexuality with a certain fear of childbirth. The story climaxes in a frightening sexual clinch and a 'frightful, tearing shriek' from Frau Lehman followed by the 'wailing' of a baby and a cry from Sabina herself: '"Achk!" shrieked Sabina, rushing from the room' and from the intrusive, even forced sexual advances of the young man (*SKM* 42). A more subtle analysis of the violence of sexual relationships, together with a sense of the imbrication of physical with sexual aggression, is portrayed in the extraordinary unfinished tale 'A Married Man's Story'. In this story the narrator tries to explain the breakdown in his relationship with his wife and his subtle, indifferent cruelty towards her by reference to his emotionally deprived childhood. The son of a chemist, he remembers being 'hated' at school (*SS* 331), his fear of his father, and his father's habitual 'sneer' as he serves his customers, and the 'gaudy' ladies who come to his father's shop for his 'famous fivepenny pick-me-up' (*SS* 330). And the narrator remembers one customer coming into the shop in desperation: 'the whole side of her face was puffed up and purple; her lip was cut and her eyelid looked as though it was gummed fast over the wet eye' (*SS* 330). This violence outside is strangely repeated within the family home where, on the night of her death, his mother comes to him – or he dreams she comes to him – and claims that his father has poisoned her. The story implies that there is a connection between this murder – if that is what it is – and the fact that after his wife's death the boy's father is free to entertain his customers as the boy lies awake upstairs. This strangely ominous narrative – Mansfield's darkest, her 'strangest' and 'most impenetrable' story, according to C. K. Stead, and one of her 'most compelling' in its 'remorselessly sinister quality' (*CR* 168) – powerfully suggests an insidious connection, once again, between violence and sexuality.

Questions of gender identification and of sexuality, then, are complex, disputed aspects of Mansfield's stories, 'queer' even, queering the figuration of writing and life. Gender and sexuality are fictions, we might say, aspects of Mansfield's sense of impersonation, never entirely stable or fixed, never quite belonging to a single identity and always subject to exploitation and abuse, open to danger and violence. Mansfield's feminism, if we can call it that, is complex and unstable, disturbing, troubled, finally inconclusive.

6

'The grass was blue': 'Prelude' and 'At the Bay'

Mansfield's first great New Zealand story, 'Prelude', was originally titled 'The Aloe'. In its final form there stands at its centre the image of the aloe, one of the strange new plants that Kezia comes across as she wanders in the family's new garden. The plant not only looks strange but, as Kezia's mother tells her, has a strange and for her mother strangely attractive reproductive life, only flowering once every hundred years. The aloe appears elsewhere in Mansfield's work, but a comment from Walter Pater's chapter on 'The Poetry of Michelangelo' in *The Renaissance* seems to suggest that the plant had a literary as well as a personal resonance for Mansfield: 'A certain strangeness, something of the blossoming of the aloe,' remarks Pater, 'is indeed an element in all true works of art: that they shall excite or surprise us is indispensable'.[1] Surprise, in the form of strangeness and 'queerness', was central to Mansfield's sense of her own work. The point is made in a letter of 25 March 1915 as she was beginning work on 'The Aloe': writing from Paris to Murry, Mansfield likens her story to the 'grotesque' shapes of boats 'dancing' on the water in the dark, 'with people rather dark and seen strangely as they move in the sharp light and shadow': 'Its queer stuff', she remarks of her story (*CLKM* i. 168). In another letter to Murry written six years later in January 1921, she comments on her sequel to 'The Aloe'/'Prelude', 'At the Bay': 'I have written a huge long story of a rather new kind,' she tells Murry, 'its the outcome of the Prelude method – it just unfolds and opens.' Again, the story is characterized in Mansfield's mind by its strangeness: 'Its a queer tale, though,' she remarks (*CLKM* iv. 156).

Referring to 'Prelude' and 'At the Bay', Elizabeth Bowen writes of Mansfield's 'august, peaceful New Zealand stories' (*CR* 75). The two stories, with their elaborate contrapuntal structures, are often construed as Mansfield's most accomplished works. The stories are both set in New Zealand and centre around the Burnell family, a family that is clearly inspired by Mansfield's memories of her Beauchamp childhood. 'They would be miracles of memory', comments Bowen, 'if one considered them memories at all'. Rather, she suggests, the stories are 'a re-living'. They are, Bowen goes on, Mansfield's 'solution' (*CR* 75).[2] The stories are Mansfield's 'solution', we might suggest, to the problem of narrative form in the short story. Rather differently, they are her resolution of writing with memory. Both 'Prelude' and 'At the Bay' are considerably longer than any of Mansfield's other stories – at fifty pages and forty pages respectively they stretch the limits of the short story form almost to breaking point. Together with other fictions focused on the Burnell family – 'How Pearl Button was Kidnapped', 'The Little Girl', 'The Doll's House', and others[3] – they may be said to constitute a kind of New Zealand Bildungsroman. Indeed, Mansfield may have intended them as the basis for a 'serial novel' that she was planning entitled *Karori*.[4] Both stories are ensemble pieces, focusing on the family group and with a perspective that shifts seamlessly, almost imperceptibly, from one character to another. And both are divided into twelve sections whose oblique, indirect linking with each other was, as Andrew Gurr comments, 'original in fiction' and most closely associated with the form of T. S. Eliot's nearly contemporary poem *The Waste Land* (1922) (*CR* 201). The importance of the two stories for Mansfield herself was marked by the fact that each was chosen to open one of the two major collections that Mansfield published in her lifetime: 'Prelude' opens *Bliss and Other Stories*, while 'At the Bay' opens *The Garden Party and Other Stories*. Both stories are concerned with the uncanny confabulation of the familiar with the unfamiliar, the homely with the unhomely, since both are concerned with ways in which the familiarity of family life, of the life of the home, is also, in a certain respect, unfamiliar, unhomely. In this sense, Mansfield seeks to 'defamiliarize' her topic, family life – itself an abiding concern in her work, from the caustic critique of German families and the German love of family in *In a German Pension* onwards.

First published as a separate volume by Virginia and Leonard Woolf's Hogarth Press in July 1918, 'Prelude' is based on the removal of the Beauchamp family from the suburbs of Wellington to a Karori country house when Mansfield was just 5 years old. Each of the twelve short, finely crafted sections focuses on and is focused through the experience of members of the Burnell family. Indeed, it is in this story that Mansfield first fully develops her mode of impersonation, what she refers to as a 'merging' of herself with the character. In a note to the manuscript of 'The Aloe', Mansfield explains that her aim is to 'get at' her characters and their ideas and predicaments 'through' those characters themselves so that she will be able to take a character such as Linda in 'Prelude' and 'suddenly merge her into herself'.[5] A letter to Dorothy Brett dated 11 October 1917 and written in the enthusiasm of having completed the story elaborates on this idea of merging a character into herself but also on the idea that the author herself 'merges' into the character or the object of her story. In this letter Mansfield describes her 'miracles of memory', supporting Bowen's sense that Mansfield's memories of a lost childhood are hardly memories at all. This, as Bowen comments, is Mansfield's 'solution': 'It seems to me so extraordinarily right', Mansfield remarks to the painter Brett, 'that you should be painting Still Lives just now':

> What can one do, faced with this wonderful tumble of round bright fruits, but gather them and play with them – and *become them*, as it were. When I pass the apple stalls I cannot help stopping and staring until I feel that I, myself, am changing into an apple, too – and that at any moment I may produce an apple, miraculously, out of my own being like the conjurer produces the egg [...] When I write about ducks I swear that I am a white duck with a round eye, floating in a pond fringed with yellow blobs and taking an occasional dart at the other duck with the round eye, which floats upside down beneath me. In fact this whole process of becoming the duck [...] is so thrilling that I can hardly breathe, only to think about it. For although that is as far as most people can get, it is really only the 'prelude'. There follows the moment when you are more duck, more apple or more Natasha than any of these objects could ever possibly be, and so you create them anew [...] But that is why I believe in

technique, too [...] I do, just because I don't see how art is going to make that divine *spring* into the bounding outlines of things if it hasn't passed through the process of trying to become these things before recreating them.   (*CLKM* i. 330)

In this revealing description of her working method, as well as giving us a clue to the significance of the title, 'Prelude', Mansfield elaborates her sense of what we are calling 'impersonations', and suggests that they may have nothing to do with persons. Impersonations involve taking on the identities of apples or of ducks as much as the adoption of human, characterological perspectives. Mansfield's use of the duck as an example is particularly intriguing, since 'Prelude' famously includes a scene in which the children are invited by Pat, the handyman, to watch him behead a white duck (the duck is later eaten at the family dinner). In this context, Mansfield's declaration that she identifies with the duck might allow us to think of her work as a kind of authorial auto-decapitation: the effect of Mansfield's 'technique' in 'Prelude' is to merge the narrative voice with that of characters or objects in the story and thus produce a kind of 'beheading', an 'impersonation' of character in which narrative or authorial voice disappears. The technique is peculiarly unsettling for the reader, leaving her to make connections, to draw conclusions, to unravel knots or nodes of meaning and significance without the guidance of the author or narrator. Indeed, it is precisely this decapitation – the excision of authorial commentary – that Mansfield worked on as she revised 'Prelude' from its original incarnation as 'The Aloe', deleting and revising moments of authorial intrusion and authorial commentary, restraining her prose and limiting her perspective to that of her characters. This, in a sense, *is* the strangeness of Mansfield's new work, of 'Prelude'.

'Prelude' concerns a series of 'moments' in which the world is created 'anew', in which human experience is structured by surprise, in which the familiar, the family and the family home, become unfamiliar and unhomely. The story focuses around the experiences of the Burnell children – with a particular focus on Mansfield's alter ego, Kezia – on the day that the family move house and the next day. The children's experiences are juxtaposed or interweaved with those of their parents, with their aunt Beryl and with their grandmother, Mrs Fairfield. The children's father, Stanley Burnell, is a somewhat naive man, driven by work and overbearing in manner, who is also sympathetic, loving, loyal, and emotionally dependent on his wife, Linda. Linda herself is remote and somewhat unloving as a mother, fearful of childbirth – though apparently pregnant for the fourth time – and both repulsed by and tender towards her husband. Beryl, Linda's vain and superficial younger sister, has unfulfilled romantic yearnings but is sexually insecure: she seems unable to help being flirtatious with men – not least with her sister's husband, Stanley – but she also despises herself for what she recognizes as her superficiality. Mrs Fairfield – Linda and Beryl's mother – is past the concerns of sex, marriage, and romantic dreams of love. She is the largely silent maternal presence that grounds the family but also, and as will become clear in 'At the Bay', ungrounds it in her proximity to death.[6] While 'Prelude' may be called an 'ensemble piece', the connections between people increasingly seem to disassemble, the story involves relationships that unfailingly fail to work. Mansfield is concerned as much with the disfunctioning of the family as with its functioning, and as much with the disunity (signified not least by the divisions of the story) as with the unity of her narrative. Above all, Mansfield's story is about the strangeness of a new world, and the strangeness embedded within what is, one might think, most familiar – family life.

This sense of strangeness is established early on. If the story revolves around the removal of the Burnell family to a new house, it is in effect, for the children, a move to a new world. Towards the beginning of the story, for example, as Kezia and her sister Lottie make their way to the new house in 'unknown country' (SS 84) in the settling dusk, the world is transformed: 'Everything looked different – the painted wooden houses far smaller than they did by day, the gardens far bigger and wilder' (SS 83); as they approach the 'soft white bulk' of the new house it seems to lay 'stretched upon the green garden like a sleeping beast' (SS 85). The children are constantly being surprised by what they see and by what they experience. Kezia sees that the handyman, Pat, is wearing ear-rings, for example: 'She never knew that men wore ear-rings. She was very much surprised' (SS 109. On seeing the aloe, she is told that it flowers only once every hundred years: 'She had never seen anything like it

61

before' (SS 98). The garden, in which she thinks she will never 'not get lost', is full of plants that 'she had never seen before' (SS 97). Three of the characters in the story – Kezia, Linda, Beryl – dream of surprising those to whom they are close. Kezia often makes 'surprises' for her grandmother and thinks about handing her a matchbox with flowers inside instead of matches (SS 98). Linda's surprise is altogether more disturbing. Her ambivalent feelings towards her husband and her sense of emotional anaesthesia towards the children form the core – the matrix – of the family's relationships and of the story itself. It is Linda's unspoken connubial ambivalence – she despises her husband, feels affection for him and pities him – together with its corollary, her maternal indifference, that may be said to structure all relationships and to determine the family's unfamiliarity with itself. At one point, Linda's ambivalence is presented, literally, as a fantasy of surprise: Linda would like to surprise her husband with the revelation that she hates him. She imagines wrapping up her feelings 'in little packets' and giving them to Stanley: 'She longed to hand him that last one' – the one she thinks of as 'this other, this hatred' – 'for a surprise': 'She could see his eyes as he opened that...' (SS 115–16). Beryl also fantasizes about revealing her 'true' self, about revealing her true emotions. She thinks that if her friend Nan Pym were presented with her 'real self' – vain, shallow, spiteful – rather than the false, flirtatious mask that she presents and the false, ingratiating voice with which she habitually speaks, her friend would 'jump out of the window with surprise' (SS 118).

Surprise, then – the revelation of the unknown, the unexpected, the unfamiliar, in what we think we know, in our homes or gardens, in our worlds, in our families or friends – inhabits the Burnell world in powerful and disturbing ways. But Mansfield is also concerned, more generally, with how things look different from themselves or how things look different from what one might expect, both for the story's characters and for its readers. She is concerned, in other words, to articulate, to play on or perform, a certain surprise and a certain strangeness in writing. The white duck, beheaded and cooked and served up for dinner, 'did not look as if it had ever had a head', for example, and has an unexpected consciousness of having been cooked: 'It lay, in beautifully basted resignation, on a blue dish'

(*SS* 112). It is not clear who thinks this or, indeed, whether any of the characters perceive it. Indeed, the same may be said for the comment that follows, where we are told that it is not only the duck that seems to have been basted, but also the cook, Alice: 'It was hard to say which of the two, Alice or the duck, looked the better basted; they were both such a rich colour and they both had the same air of gloss and strain' (*SS* 112). The experience of strangeness here, as at other points in the story, is not tied to the perception of any particular person, but floats free of characterological identification. And there is a quiet, almost imperceptible slippage from the characters' to the readers' encounter with strangeness, with the unfamiliar.

In her letter to Brett, Mansfield enthusiastically describes the 'unspeakable thrill of this art business' and her 'intense' 'longing to serve my subject as well as I can' (*CLKM* i. 331). She describes the inspiration for 'Prelude', her 'perfect passion' for the 'island where I was born':

> in the early morning there I always remember feeling that this little island has dipped back into the dark blue sea during the night only to rise again at beam of day, all hung with bright spangles and glittering drops – (When you ran over the dewy grass you positively felt that your feet tasted salt.) I tried to catch that moment – with something of its sparkle and its flavour. And just as on those mornings white milky mists rise and uncover some beauty, then smother it again and then again disclose it. I tried to lift that mist from my people and let them be seen and then to hide them again... (*CLKM* i. 331).

The comments give a powerful sense of the newness of colonial New Zealand, the strangeness of what is for Mansfield an eternally new, eternally renewed country. But in its evocation of the early morning, the sea, the mist, and the dewy grass, and in its hallucinatory, dreamlike perception of nature, the letter also seems to prefigure the opening to Mansfield's second great New Zealand story, 'At the Bay', which was not in fact written until four years later.[7] Mansfield's concern in her later story seems to be even more strongly bound up in the desire to re-*create* the world of her memory, her New Zealand childhood. In another letter to Brett, this time written while working on 'At the Bay' in August 1921, Mansfield imagines her later story to be 'full of sand and seaweed and bathing dresses hanging over verandahs

& sandshoes on window sills, and little pink "sea" convolvulus, and rather gritty sandwiches and the tide coming in. And it smells', she hopes, 'a little bit fishy' (*CLKM* iv. 261). Writing to her friend again a few weeks later she refers to 'that very long seaweedy story of mine' and jokes that she feels 'inclined to suggest' to her editors that they 'give away a spade an' bucket with each copy' (*CLKM* iv. 295).

'At the Bay' returns to the Burnell family and describes a single summer day spent in the family's holiday cottage on Crescent Bay. Once again the story is divided into numbered sections and the deftly drawn characters of 'Prelude' are developed and added to. Jonathan Trout, the husband of Linda's sister, is introduced. Jonathan is frustrated with work and lacking ambition. His idealistic, playful but ultimately disappointed sense of the possibilities that life has to offer contrasts strikingly with the irritable, emotionally fragile, but work-obsessed Stanley Burnell. Mrs Harry Kember, a masculinized, cigarette-smoking advocate of sensuous fulfilment, of living for the moment, is introduced as a dangerous friend of Beryl. Beryl's romantic longings are the focus of the final section of the story and come to an unexpected climax as she is disturbingly propositioned by Harry Kember. Alice, the servant, has her own scene, in which she makes a social call and reveals her own vanities and social aspirations (the scene is deftly drawn but Mansfield later referred to it as one of the 'big black holes' of the story (*LKM* ii. 201)). The Samuel Josephs children, who also made a brief appearance in 'Prelude' figure as teasing and threatening peers of the Burnell girls, while the Trout boys, Pip and Rags, again take their part as the girls' playmates. Linda's fierce desire for solitude and privacy, her 'dread of having children' (*SS* 295) is re-emphasized and reinforced by the fact that she has now given birth to a baby son towards whom she feels detached. And yet, in section six, she also begins to experience something 'new' towards him, a surprise for her, something that makes tears 'dance' in her eyes (*SS* 296), something, we can surmise, approaching love.

Just as 'Prelude' is structured by moments of strangeness, what seems at times to be the hymn to childhood of 'At the Bay' is structured by the strangeness constituted by a more insistent sense of potential physical, psychological, and sexual violence, figured in and as an uneasy relationship between reality and fantasy. Jonathan Trout's idyllic morning swim, for example, ends badly when, having stayed in the sea too long, he begins to turn 'blue with cold' and to 'ache all over': 'it was as though some one was wringing the blood out of him' (*SS* 285). After Stanley Burnell leaves for work, all the women in the house feel a sense of relief and Alice, washing up, holds a teapot under water 'as if it too was a man and drowning was too good for them' (*SS* 288). The insinuating Mrs Harry Kember – with her subversive smoking habit, her bridge playing, her ability to lie 'in the full glare of the sun', the 'long, strange-looking woman with narrow hands and feet', the woman with a face 'long and narrow and exhausted-looking' and her hair 'burnt out and withered' (*SS* 291–2), with her homoerotic commentary on Beryl's body, and with her questionable gender identity – turns into a poisonous rat: 'And suddenly she turned turtle, disappeared, and swam away quickly, quickly, like a rat [...] Beryl felt that she was being poisoned by this cold woman [...] how strange how horrible!' (*SS* 294). Indeed, she gives the other women at the bay violent thoughts. They seem to take comfort in the idea of her untimely death: thinking of her husband as someone who would 'commit a murder one day', they imagine her 'stretched as she lay on the beach; but cold, bloody, and still with a cigarette stuck in the corner of her mouth' (*SS* 292). Kezia is told about death by her grandmother, Mrs. Fairfield, and realizes in a moment of panic that both she herself and her beloved grandmother will die: 'This was awful. "Promise me you won't ever do it, grandma," ' pleads Kezia (*SS* 299). Alice's friend, the widowed Mrs Stubbs turns out to be disturbingly unconcerned about her husband's death, preferring 'freedom' to matrimony, the 'queer' revelation of which, following on from the revelation of the manner of his death, makes Alice uneasy and makes her wish that she was back in her kitchen (*SS* 303). Playing in the washhouse, the Burnell children and their cousins suddenly become frightened as night falls and they hear unexplained noises. They see a face at the window – 'Pressed against the window was a pale face, black eyes, a black beard' (*SS* 306) – and there is a moment of terror and panic until the benign Jonathan Trout reveals himself. And the story ends with Beryl's dream of romance turning into horrible, farcical, and potentially violent reality as Harry Kember, ten years his wife's junior, 'incredibly handsome' but with a face 'like a mask' and like a 'man walking in his sleep', a man whom other men 'couldn't stand' (*SS* 292) and a man whom others consider capable of wife-murder, comes to entice Beryl to come out for a walk – before, when she resists, calling her 'silly' and a 'cold little devil' in his 'hateful voice' (*SS* 314).

'At the Bay' is framed by set-piece descriptions that present a rather different sense of strangeness, the strangeness of the inhuman. The story opens with a three-page section that sets the scene – describing what in a letter Mansfield calls the 'incomparable beauty of very early morning, before human beings are awake' (*CLKM* iv. 297); in its centre is a three-paragraph passage at the beginning of section seven (and thus at the centre of the story) describing the beach deserted in the midday sun; and there is a four-sentence closing paragraph that returns to the deserted, dehumanized scene of the bay at the end of the day. Mansfield's technical mastery in these descriptions is remarkable and constitutes some of her finest, most carefully wrought, and most controlled writing. Returning to the motif of strangeness and the uncanny, the first paragraph comes as a delicately phrased and carefully nuanced surprise in which, as Antony Alpers comments, 'The author, refined almost out of existence, only sees' (*L.* 344):

> Very early morning. The sun was not yet risen, and the whole of Crescent Bay was hidden under a white sea-mist. The big bush-covered hills at the back were smothered. You could not see where they ended and the paddocks and bungalows began. The sandy road was gone and the paddocks and bungalows the other side of it; there were no white dunes covered with reddish grass beyond them; there was nothing to mark which was beach and where was the sea. A heavy dew had fallen. The grass was blue. Big drops hung on the bushes and just did not fall; the silvery, fluffy toi-toi was limp on its long stalks, and all the marigolds and the pinks in the bungalow gardens were bowed to the earth with wetness. Drenched were the cold fuchsias, round pearls of dew lay on the flat nasturtium leaves. It looked as though the sea had beaten up softly in the darkness, as though one immense wave had come rippling, rippling – how far? Perhaps if you had waked up in the middle of the night you might have seen a big fish flicking in at the window and gone again (*SS* 281)

The control of syntax, diction, imagery, and rhythm in this paragraph is both remarkable and hard-won. The opening sentence – strikingly elliptical, underplayed, uninflected – itself marks a new beginning both in terms of the story itself and in terms of stylistic technique. The whole of the opening concerns itself with revelation and concealment, with appearance – and appearances – and disappearance. The second sentence describes a scene that cannot be seen, hidden, as it is, 'under a white sea-mist'. Mansfield has set herself the task of describing what 'just' cannot be seen and what 'just' does not happen: 'Big drops hung on the bushes and just did not fall' denotes an action that is heavy with anticipation but unconsummated. But disappearance – the disappearance of marks or boundaries – is not only a visual question in this opening: it is also a question of narrative voice. The opening phrase 'Very early morning' marks the absence of authorial or narrative voice, persona, position, or perspective. The visual is constituted by what cannot be seen, while at the same time the subject who perceives the scene is also veiled. Thus the disappearance of narrative voice is allied with a disappearing scene, a spectrality of the spectacle, and a withdrawal of the subject who sees. The hills, for example, are 'smothered', so that 'you' cannot see the join between hills and paddocks. But 'you' disappears – you disappear – in the next sentence (only to return towards the end of the paragraph), where we find that, continuing the dominant trope of disappearance in this opening, 'The sandy road was gone'. As the passage continues with the disappearance of the white dunes and of the join between the beach and the sea, it becomes clear that Mansfield is describing a whole world that 'just' cannot be seen, a trope of disappearance that metamorphoses into that of dream, into the dislocation of perception and the disappearance of the conscious, perceiving, human subject. While the dream sentence 'The grass was blue' has a rational or empirical, experiential explanation – the grass appears to be blue in the early morning light, drenched as it is in dew – it functions in hallucinatory opposition to perception, to spectacle. The sentence also marks a resistance to spectatorship itself (who *sees* it as blue?), a resistance that is developed in the closing sentence of the paragraph in the surreal, dream image of the fish 'flicking in at the window'. Carefully orchestrating her rhetoric and imagery, then, Mansfield opens her major narrative with a eulogy to impersonality, with the image of a dehumanized scene unobserved by any human, only perceptible from the perspective of an intricately formulated, an intricately structured textuality.

The short closing paragraph is, perhaps, even more remarkable, even more controlled, in its evocation of an unpeopled scene:

> A cloud, small, serene, floated across the moon. In that moment of darkness the sea sounded deep, troubled. Then the cloud sailed away, and the sound of the sea was a vague murmur, as though it waked out of a dark dream. All was still.   (SS 314)

To balance the restraint of the story's opening sentence – 'Very early morning' – the narrative ends with a similarly elliptical phrase: 'All was still.' But the paragraph resists the closure that stillness suggests, hinting, instead, at an apocalyptic or deathly stillness – *all* was still. It is a troubling stillness, then, like the deep of the sea and its vague murmur. What remains at the end of 'At the Bay' is an emptied scene, a scene in a certain sense not seen, one 'troubled' by itself and by its sounds, a dream scene, abandoned, deserted, unpeopled.

The strangeness of Mansfield's major stories resides, finally, in the strangeness, not least, of not being yourself, in the impersonation of impersonation, in the disappearance of persons. While both 'Prelude' and 'At the Bay' are focused around the peopled landscapes of memory and while they are structured around the evocation, the bringing to life, of people from the past in the impersonations of their voices and their perspectives, the stories also have to do with a certain narrative restraint, the impersonality of prose, the disappearance of people in acts of impersonation.

7

The 'other passion'

Katherine Mansfield hated, with a passion. Her letters, journals and stories, give a powerful sense of her delight in hatred, that most intimate, most 'personal' of emotions. Mansfield was passionate in her hatreds and passionate about hate. Bertrand Russell, writing in 1949 to disclaim an affair with Mansfield, declared that he 'admired her passionately, but was repelled by her dark hatreds'.[1] 'Hatred', comments Claire Tomalin, 'was her favourite emotion' (*SL* 6); she had, Elizabeth Bowen remarks, 'a terrifying capacity for contempt'.[2] Mansfield's notebooks and letters often express her hatreds and include a number of reflections on the passion. 'I hate everybody, loathe myself, loathe my Life,' she declares decisively in an early notebook entry (*KMN* i. 101); 'No, I hate society,' in a later entry (*KMN* i. 282). 'People are vile', she tells Brett, 'but Life *is* thrilling' (*CLKM* ii. 170). But then later, as if her hatred is not hers, 'I don't want to hate people: I want to love them' (*CLKM* ii. 260). She even contemplates writing a story on the topic. 'I'd like to write a *long long* story on this & call it "Last Words to Life". One *ought* to write it, and another on the subject of HATE' (*KMN* ii. 180). Occasionally she will simply expostulate on 'her' hatred in the abstract: 'Oh, my *hatred!*' she declares in one notebook (*KMN* ii. 295). But often it is more focused: 'Oh how I *loathe* hotels,' she tells Ottoline Morrell (*CLKM* ii. 192), and she writes to Murry on housework that 'I hate hate HATE doing these things that you accept just as all men accept of their women' (*CLKM* i. 125). On a personal level, it was for her companion Ida Baker ('L.M.') that, as her letters and notebooks make clear, Mansfield reserved her most virulent hatred: 'shes a revolting hysterical ghoul,' she writes of her friend in a characteristically hysterical outburst, 'Shes never content except when she can eat me' (*CLKM* ii. 68).

'Its not the slightest use pretending I can stand people,' she remarks in a letter to Murry, 'I *cant*. I hate L.M. so utterly and detest *her* so that shes torture' (*CLKM* ii. 109). 'My love for her is so divided by my extreme *hate* for her', she remarks later, 'that I really think the latter has it' (*CLKM* ii. 190). In another notebook entry she expounds at some length on the topic of hatred and on a long conversation that she has had with Baker: 'I must not forget the long talk Ida & I had the other evening about *hate*', she tells herself: 'What is hate? Who has even described it? Why do I feel it for her?', she goes on (*KMN* ii. 325). It is not difficult to see why Brigid Brophy could think that the 'crisis' of Mansfield's personality involved the question of 'how to govern a furious impulse of aggression' and that the 'impulse' in all her best writing is 'cruelty' (*CR* 89–90).[3]

In 'Prelude', Linda imagines doing up her feelings in 'little packets' and giving them to her husband, Stanley. The last packet that she would give him would surprise him: it would contain what she calls 'this other, this hatred' (*SS* 115–16). In a letter to Murry of November 1919 Mansfield uses a similar expression as she dwells at length on the experience of hatred. For Mansfield, hatred placed her apart and made her what she was – hatred that her husband, finally, was unable to share, was unable to understand. 'My black fit is on me,' she tells Murry:

> Christ! To *hate* like I do. Its upon me today. You don't know what hatred is because I know you have never hated anyone – not as you have loved – equally. Thats what I do. My deadly deadly enemy has got me today and Im simply a blind force of hatred. Hate is the *other* passion. It has all the opposite effects of Love. It fills you with death and corruption. It makes you feel hideous degraded and old – it makes you long to DESTROY. Just as the other is light so this is darkness. I hate like that – a million times multiplied. Its like being under a curse. (*CLKM* iii. 105)

While Mansfield's sense of hatred as the 'other passion' is clearly intended to indicate its difference from, its opposition to, the passion of love, there is also a sense here that hatred is other to the self that hates. Hatred is 'simply a blind force' and it has its own independent existence, independent from the subject who hates: hatred is itself hated as Mansfield's 'deadly deadly enemy'. Hatred is an experience or emotion that 'gets' Mansfield, that has its own volition, and that dissociates her from *her* volition, like a curse. But there is also a joy in hating, a pleasure taken from visceral, irrational, un-just hatred, and sometimes one can sense the delight that Mansfield feels in her emotion. Her hatred can look like pure and unashamed prejudice: 'I hate fat people,' she declares in one letter (*CLKM* ii. 77). At other times, the prejudice is for a place or nationality – England especially: 'All day I was possessed by my hate of England,' she writes in one notebook during her affair with Francis Carco: 'It is after him my one passion – a loathing for England' (*KMN* ii. 5); and again, in a letter to Brett, 'How I have hated England [...] It's a kind of *negation* to me' (*CLKM* iv. 255). At other times, hatred becomes theorized as part of a more complex political and social philosophy, and the First World War had a profound influence on Mansfield in this respect. Writing towards the end of the war, for example, Mansfield considers fallen humanity as she contemplates childhood, with an appalled sense of children's inhumanity to children that foreshadows that of, for example, William Golding in *Lord of the Flies*:

> I wonder what *is* going to happen. If the war will end in our lives – but even if it does end human beings will still be as vile as ever – I think there is something in the idea that children are born in sin, judging from the hateful little wretches who 'play' under my window somehow – horrible little toads – just as evil as slum children – just as mean as french children – I believe if they were left to themselves the strong ones would kill the weak 'uns – torture them – and jump on them until they were flat! Well, that's excusable in grownup people – but in children...! Oh, people are ugly – I have such a contempt for them – How hideous they are – and what a mess they have made of everything. It can never be cleared up & I haven't the least desire to take even a feather duster to it. Let it be – & let it kill them – which it WONT do [...] one must have an iron shutter over ones heart. (*CLKM* ii. 188)

The passage involves a remarkable articulation of hatred, figuring it as spreading from children 'playing' under her window (where the venomous inverted commas suggest that such play is anything but playful), to slum children, to the French, to people in general. Mansfield's diatribe – specifically because of its passionate unreason – gives a strong sense of the poisonous, miasmic nature of hatred, the way that it spreads, uncontainably.

As with other early twentieth-century writers – D. H. Lawrence, T. S. Eliot, Ezra Pound, Wyndham Lewis, for example – this passion, this hatred, developed at times into a quasi-Nietzschean hatred of the masses that flirts with the politics of hatred, with fascism: 'Truly one must hate humankind in the mass – hate them as passionately as one loves the few – the very few,' Mansfield remarks in another letter (*CLKM* ii. 339).

Hatred may be said to be the driving force behind the stories collected in Mansfield's first book, *In a German Pension*, a book that skates, as C. K. Stead remarks, 'on very thin ice': the laughter of the book, Stead comments, is 'right at the brink of hysteria, tears, revulsion and hatred' (*CR* 157). The hatreds of *In a German Pension* are focused on the middle-aged German bourgeoisie, on their conversation, their clothes, their men (especially), their sexual relationships, their eating habits and digestion, their interest in their eating habits and digestion, their respectability and their snobbery, their families and their love of family, their language, their Germanness, their crass, amoral indifference. Indeed, hatred may be said to impel *In a German Pension*, arguably to its detriment: with its intrusive and opinionated author-narrator, its insistence on emphasizing the coarse, hateful Bavarian bourgeoisie, its sarcasm and cutting, pointed irony, the book has, for many readers, a strictly limited interest. It is, of course, precisely this intrusiveness, this personalized authorial direction, this naked, undisguised spite, that Mansfield restrains in her later more successful stories, that she develops into an authorial merging with character – into impersonation. And this merging, this impersonation in the later stories, undercuts any easy sense of moral exteriority or superiority on the part of the author or in fact the reader.[4] Nevertheless, as Bowen, Brophy, Tomalin, and others suggest, hatred may be said to be a theme – or a literary effect – that permeates all of Mansfield's writing, not just her first book, and that, indeed, may be said to structure and focus many of her narratives. As Malcolm Cowley remarked in a review of *Bliss*, Mansfield is more likely to write about 'people she dislikes' than about those 'she finds agreeable'. *Bliss*, he goes on, in a somewhat melodramatic analogue, is 'a book of neurotics; a literary corridor of the psychopathic ward': 'wherever her sympathy does not lead her to understanding,' he observes, 'her hate does' (*CR* 5).[5] Thus 'Mr Reginald Peacock's Day', for example, focuses on what Cowley calls a 'venomously meticulous account' of one character's day (*CR* 5), featuring a man who seems to be impelled by hatred, while forms of hatred are expressed and hate-filled characters appear in 'The Man without a Temperament', 'Feuille d'Album', 'The Little Governess', 'The Escape', 'Prelude', 'At the Bay', 'The Young Girl', 'Her First Ball', 'A Married Man's Story', and many others.

One of Mansfield's most accomplished stories, 'Je ne parle pas français', may be said to be constructed around hatred, and an analysis of this fiction might help to give a final perspective on the question of Mansfield's writing, in particular on her work of impersonation, on its difficulties and risks. On 3–4 February 1918, while working on the story, Mansfield wrote a letter to Murry describing it in some detail. But since Murry is himself a probable target of the satire as the model for Dick Harmon, the letter is almost comic in its desire for approval ('I am so EXCEEDINGLY anxious for your opinion [. . .] Oh God – is it good?', she asks Murry), its assurance that she is not writing 'with a sting' ('Im not, indeed!', she exclaims), nor from 'life' ('Theres so much much less taken from life than anybody would credit'), and at the same time its desire to reveal her inspiration (one paragraph ends in the incomplete sentence 'Dick Harmon of course is partly is', emphatically failing to say *who* he is) (*CLKM* ii.56). On 3 February she had written to Murry an eloquent account of her inspirations, what she called her two 'kick offs' in the 'writing game', one of which is 'joy – real joy' while the other is *not* 'hate or destruction' exactly but an '*extremely* deep sense of hopelessness', a '*cry against corruption*' (*CLKM* ii. 54). It is this 'cry against corruption', she suggests, that has inspired 'Je ne parle pas français'. As Claire Tomalin has commented, however, the idea that the story is a 'cry against corruption' bears 'little relation to the work' in question, which is really about a 'voyeuristic but fairly harmless gigolo and an act of treachery committed by a character easily recognizable as Murry himself' (*SL* 168–9). I would like to suggest that it is Mansfield's complex denial in her letter to Murry – her denial that the story has a 'sting', her denial that it is taken from 'life', and her denial that her inspiration is 'hatred' – that gives us a clue to the nature of her story. In other words, I want to suggest that we might read the story as a narrative inspired by, about, hatred. We might agree with Virginia Woolf when she comments that the story 'breathes nothing but hate',[6] or with Mary Burgan that the hatred is focused on homosexuality in this, Mansfield's 'most homophobic story'.[7]

'Je ne parle pas français' involves a partly repressed, partly articulated hatred – including self-hatred – that not only dominates the narrator's thoughts but may also be said to constitute the proper, the required response to his character. The story is told from the perspective of a world-weary, darkly damaged writer, Raoul Duquette, who, as a 10-year-old child was sexually abused by his family's African laundress. Duquette is a Parisian intellectual, a lover of English literature, a male prostitute, and a pimp who spends his time in cafés observing, with satiric detachment, other clientèle. This portrait of the venomous writer is, Mansfield claimed in a letter, a portrait of her friends Francis Carco and Mark Gertler – '& God knows who', she adds (*CLKM* ii. 56). Included within the phrase '& God knows who' is, we might surmise, the writer herself, for the portrait is, most importantly, a displaced self-portrait. There is, to confirm our sense of the troubled self-reflexivity of the portrait, a letter that depicts Mansfield herself as Duquette-like in habits: Mansfield wrote the story between late January and early February 1918, but writing to Murry a few weeks later in a letter from Paris dated 18 March 1918 she describes herself sitting in a café 'drinking & looking at the mirrors & smoking and thinking how utterly corrupt life is – how hideous human beings are' (*CLKM* ii. 129).[8] In this respect, the story may be read as what Tomalin calls 'a deeply subversive signal about [Mansfield's] own complex nature' (*SL* 170). And part of the subversion may be understood to involve Mansfield's representation of the paradoxes and risks inherent in her writing, inherent in acts of literary impersonation.

Like Mansfield, Duquette is sceptical about the stability and individuality of personality. His view of human life is encapsulated in the second paragraph of the story: he does not, he tells us, believe in 'the mystery of the human soul' because he does not believe in 'the human soul'. Instead, he sees people as being like 'portmanteaux – packed with certain things, started going, thrown about, tossed away, dumped down, lost and found, half emptied suddenly, or squeezed fatter than ever' (*SS* 142). This scepticism concerning the unity of the 'soul' is indeed evinced in Duquette's verbal mannerisms, in the fracturing of his own rhetoric. He regularly undermines his own comments and seems to suffer from a disease of self-consciousness whereby his cynicism concerning others is turned on himself, as if his self is a portmanteau, packed with conflicting things. In the following exchange, for example, Duquette's world-weary cynicism is reflected back on the heteroglossia of his own crass writing style:

> QUERY. Why am I so bitter against Life? And why do I see her as a rag-picker on the American cinema, shuffling along wrapped in a filthy shawl with her old claws crooked over a stick?
> ANSWER. The direct result of the American cinema acting upon a weak mind. (*SS* 143)

As the passage suggests, Duquette has an ingrained habit of employing extravagant metaphor and hackneyed cliché and then commenting on his own prose in a kind of linguistic or literary self-hatred, a hate-filled consciousness concerning the very texture of his own writing – 'Anyhow, the "short winter afternoon was drawing to a close," as they say,' he opens the next paragraph, with disabling self-consciousness (143). Similarly, after a paragraph ending in the incongruous image of the Virgin Mary entering a Parisian café, he spends some time anxiously revealing the artfully constructed nature of his prose: 'That's rather nice, don't you think, that bit about the Virgin? It comes from the pen so gently; it has such a "dying fall". I thought so at the time and decided to make a note of it. One never knows when a little tag like that may come in useful to round off a paragraph' (*SS* 144). There is a self-reflexive self-disgust here but also a disgust at the very self-reflexivity of the gesture. But this brings us to the unavoidable paradox of Mansfield's impersonations. Sydney Kaplan argues that 'Je ne parle pas français' parodies the 'self-centredness of some of [Mansfield's] modernist contemporaries',[9] but what it also necessarily comments on is itself: in this story it is the comments on writing that are themselves the most hate-filled, most self-disgusted aspects of the writing. There is a troubling sense, in other words, that the expression of self-hatred cannot help but infect, miasmically, Mansfield's writing, since her voice, her very language, is embedded within, is encompassed by, Duquette's. As Kaplan remarks, Mansfield's critique is 'as much about herself as it is about Duquette': Mansfield parodies with a 'ruthless thrust' her own tendency towards self-analysis and self-admiration.[10] This is the risk of Mansfield's technique of impersonation, of her merging of her voice with that of her narrator, but it is also its achievement. Mansfield's achievement is highly paradoxical: by merging her own voice with that of Duquette, by *fundamentally* collapsing the distinction between authorial and narrative voice, or by making that distance uncertain, undecidable, Mansfield also finally collapses the distinction between what we might think of, what we might experience, as hatred for Duquette's writing and hatred for her own.

The story of 'Je ne parle pas français', developed over thirty pages, is minimal, and much of the interest – Duquette's as much as ours – is focused on the character of the narrator. Duquette notices the title words of the story, 'Je ne parle pas français', on a blotting pad supplied by the café. On seeing the scribbled words, he experiences a modernist or Proustian moment of revelation, of epiphany. Even here, though, a certain disconcerting self-consciousness undercuts the significance of the experience. Duquette feels himself dissolving in the intensity of the moment of revelation, feels 'overcome', 'dissolved, melted, turned into water'. Rather than revelation, however, the passage seems to end in the blindness of Duquette's self-conscious self-importance. Unwittingly evoking the pomposity of the fox in the nursery tale of 'The Three Little Pigs', Mansfield's narrator also banalizes the rhetoric of aposeopesis in the pause before the semantic emptiness of the paragraph's last word: 'And I puffed and puffed, blowing off finally with: "After all I must be first-rate. No second-rate mind could have experienced such an intensity of feeling so... purely"' (SS 145). The words 'Je ne parle pas français' remind Duquette of an incident from his past, involving his relationship with an English friend Dick Harmon. Duquette, we can surmise, experiences a certain homoerotic fascination towards Harmon: 'All the while we were together Dick never went with a woman,' Duquette tells us, 'I sometimes wondered whether he wasn't completely innocent' (SS 152). To Duquette's dismay, Harmon suddenly leaves Paris but then later returns with an English woman, 'Mouse', with whom he has eloped. Duquette acts as a kind of procurer for Harmon and Mouse by meeting them on their arrival and accompanying them to the hotel rooms that he has arranged for them. The sense that Harmon himself is troubled by his own sexuality is confirmed by the fact that he immediately abandons the woman with the explanation that their relationship would upset his mother. The woman tells Duquette that her character has been compromised by her liaison with Harmon and by their elopement and declares that she cannot return to England. But she also denies – in French, paradoxically – that she can speak French: 'Je ne parle pas français.' 'That was her swan song for me' (SS 166), the narrator remarks, incongruously. Although he promises to return to the hotel the next day to help her, Duquette also abandons Mouse by failing to return, and we are left to surmise the fate of a young woman without French or money alone in Paris and unable to return home. But Duquette's own life is of more interest to him. He ends his story with an insight into the seedy Parisian underworld that he inhabits, where he gives his 'word of honour' – 'as a gentleman, a writer, serious, young, and extremely interested in modern English literature' – that the girls that he procures for 'dirty old gallant[s]' are virgins (SS 167).[11] Duquette's preposterous and farcical sense of self-importance, articulated not least in his literary ambitions – and undercut by the titles of his books, *False Coins*, *Wrong Doors*, *Left Umbrellas* – are at the centre of this narrative's expression of hatred and self-hatred. What we are calling hatred is directed at a certain kind of writing and a certain kind of literary life, but cannot avoid also being directed at elements of Mansfield's own writing and her own life.

As in many other stories, but perhaps more strikingly and disturbingly here, Mansfield plays ambiguously within the space between her own voice and that of her despicable narrator. As we have seen, one of the key technical advances that Mansfield makes in the mode of the short story concerns her development of narrative impersonation. In this case, the result is a narrative of hatred and disgust,[12] a narrative in which hatred and self-hatred are the dominant motifs: Duquette hates and is disgusted with Parisian life, with himself, with other people. But this narrative of hatred is also one that can inspire something very similar to hatred – even as Burgan suggests, a kind of homophobia – in the reader. It is easy to hate, to feel disgust at Duquette, his narrative, his language. The risk that Mansfield takes is that we will feel repelled not just by Duquette, but by her story, which is, after all, 'his' story. Mansfield presents us with something of a paradox or aporia – a certain effect of undecidability, even unreadability: we are left with the question of the extent to which her own prose is itself caught up in this play of hatred and self-hatred. Indeed, the story may be said to involve Mansfield's impersonation of herself as a repellent other. In this respect, it may be too simple to argue that the narrative is homophobic (Duquette is, after all, bisexual rather than homosexual) except with respect to the extent to which the word 'homophobia' includes not just fear and hatred of homosexuals but also, more properly in an etymological sense, a hatred of the same, of the self. This makes, of course, for unequivocally uneasy reading. What might be called the normal protocols of reading – which include certain identifications and certain ethical judgements – are necessarily suspended and we are left not only in a state of uncertainty but also with a certain sense of hatred, even self-hatred. It is difficult to laugh at or with this narrator, yet difficult not to. It is difficult to feel sympathy for the abandoned woman – who is little more than a cipher – but difficult not to feel that the story hints at a certain ethics of compassion. It is difficult, except in a spirit of Duquettian narcissism and nihilism, to accept the narrator's sweeping disregard for humankind but difficult to feel secure in dismissing his account. The clichéd texture and the self-reflexive distancing mechanisms through which the narrative is told, its superficiality, its hackneyed phraseology and conception, resist any attempt to probe the tale for moral or hermeneutic profundity, and the morally attenuated responses of the narrator unground our desire for ethical certainty. In one of Mansfield's most extraordinary and in many ways most difficult fictions, then, the miasma of hatred becomes a certain self-hatred. Hatred, we might say – and this is the point, this is the radical challenge that Mansfield's work produces – becomes part of the experience of reading 'Je ne parle pas français'. The story plays out Mansfield's sense of hatred as the 'other passion' and reveals more starkly than her other stories the difficulty and the risks involved in articulating the troubled relationship between personality and impersonation.

8

Conclusion: Interruption

Increasingly towards the end of her short, interrupted life and as the inevitability of her early death becomes a less and less resistible conclusion, Mansfield's fictions are characterized by a sense of impermanence, of the temporary, by what Vincent O'Sullivan describes as a 'flickering of mood and atmosphere' that 'prevents any feeling or perspective from lasting more than a short time' (CR 139). While Mansfield's recognition of the brevity of life – of her life – may be one dimension of this concern with impermanence, it is also, necessarily, an aspect of her chosen form, the short story, a form that is characterized by interruption, by a breaking-off or closing-down before an end can be reached, before closure is established, or by a closing-off too early, by the banality of a 'twist in the tale'. The strangeness – the queerness – of Mansfield's fictions concerns, not least, the strangeness of ending, of conclusion, of closure. In many of Mansfield's stories, the end comes at a moment of revelation, at a moment when a character is finally able to come to understand or to express a certain truth. And yet, characteristically, these moments are undercut so that they 'just' do not occur. 'The Garden Party', for example, ends with Laura's sense that, after the success of her garden party and after confronting the dead man from the nearby workers' cottages, she has understood something: ' "Isn't life", she stammered, "isn't life – " But what life was she couldn't explain' (SS 349). 'Bliss' ends by self-consciously questioning closure, expressing uncertainty about the future, about what is going to happen now, at the end of the story, as if the end of the story may not be the end (' "Oh, what is going to happen now?" she cried', is the penultimate sentence (SS 185)). Similarly, in 'The Daughters of the Late Colonel', both daughters experience a certain revelation concerning the

79

relation between the 'other life' of helping and placating their father, on the one hand, and on the other, those times when, as Constantia thinks, 'she really felt herself'. But this revelation leads only to questions – 'What did it mean? What was it she was always wanting? What did it all lead to? Now? Now?' – and to a moment in which both daughters try but fail, finally, to verbalize this desire for a conclusion, 'now', and both end by 'forgetting' what it is they want to say (*SS* 248–9). Profundity, the revelation of a secret depth or a hidden self, is what these endings characteristically strive for but what they always, in the end, fail to express.

Mansfield's fictions, then, are concerned with and structured by a certain bathos, by the building-up of expectation in character or in reader that is then undermined by the disappointment of resolution (in both senses of 'of': Mansfield's resolutions are designed to disappoint, and she disappoints our expectations that there will be resolution). Following on from Chekhov and Gogol and writing at the same time as Joyce and Woolf, Mansfield did much to bring the short story into the modern age, to modernize it. While short stories traditionally rely on conceptually neat narrative reversals and recognitions, Mansfield often eschewed such reductive formulations or strove for a kind of dropping away, an interruption or disappointment in her endings. Indeed, disappointment for Mansfield was what daffodils were for Wordsworth or what deprivation was for Philip Larkin, an inspiration, a world view, and, in her case at least, the structuring principle on which her narratives are founded.[1] Characters in Mansfield's stories tend to wait, as Linda does, preternaturally, in 'Prelude': 'Only she seemed to be listening with her wide open watchful eyes, waiting for someone to come who just did not come, waiting for something to happen that just did not happen' (*SS* 93). Things 'just' don't happen in Mansfield: they *almost* happen, but don't; and, by contrast, they simply *don't* happen. But disappointment is also the essence of what Mansfield made of the short story, the story that, by very definition, is short, interrupted, inconclusive, something of a letdown, a falling-off.[2] Disappointment for Mansfield, we might say, constitutes a deconstruction of closure. Her short stories do not quite add up, do not quite provide what they promise. Mansfield transforms the short story genre to elaborate a poetics of lack: personal identity, narrative structure, and the so-called symbolic or symbolist dimension of the narratives all resist finality, consummation, closure. While some of her most accomplished fictions – 'A Married Man's Story', for example, or 'The Doves' Nest' – were left unfinished on her death, others that were completed end in irresolution. This quality of irresolution often makes for difficult reading – and criticism, with its concerns for the significance of a narrative whole and its resistance to inconsistency and inconsequentiality, has to develop a new vocabulary to explore and explicate Mansfield's poetics of incompletion. While David Daiches may be right when he comments that in Mansfield's stories 'Nothing is superfluous, nothing is mere decoration or trimming, everything has its part to play in producing the required effect' (*CR* 39), at the same time her stories are also impelled by irresolution, inconsequentiality, and a lack of disclosure. Mansfield's narratives often explore epiphanic moments not as revelations but as resistance to revelation, as the displacement of meaning and the suspension of sense, as the failure of resolution and the failure of language.

This structural, narrative, sense of incompletion, of interruption, even of failure, is also central to Mansfield's notion of personal identity, to her evocations of self and of selves. Thematically, Mansfield's short stories concern people whose sense of identity, whose sense of self, is, more often than not, incomplete. Her stories often concern children or adolescents, people whose identities are not yet fixed. Alternatively, they concern adults whose insecure, impermanent sense of who they are is shockingly disturbed or dislodged in often quite tragic circumstances, but in circumstances that will not allow them to regroup, to revise their sense of self, to stabilize themselves as selves. This thematic concern with the 'person', with identity and its failure, is in fact summed up in a late notebook entry as a philosophical position, as a 'philosophy' of 'the defeat of the personal' (*KMN* ii. 190). Mansfield's primary technical innovation concerns her distancing of authorial voice or persona from her narratives, her refusal to offer the comforts and certainties of authorial commentary or perspective. She allows her characters to speak for themselves – in as much as they have coherent, stable selves for which and from which to speak – and, more radically, perhaps, she structures her longer and best-known stories around a series of voices and perspectives from which narratorial or authorial voice and perspective is strictly excluded. Mansfield's impersonations, then, are the risk and the achievement of her work and of her 'double life' – of her life and of the life of her writing. It is to this risk and this achievement that Elizabeth Bowen responds, no doubt, and not only to Mansfield's early death, when she comments, in her awkward, evocative prose, that as a fellow writer she 'cannot but look at Katherine Mansfield's work as interrupted, hardly more than suspended, momentarily waiting to be gone on with' (CR 71).

Notes

CHAPTER 1. INTRODUCTION: A 'DOUBLE LIFE'

1. See C. K. Stead's account of the chronology in *CR* 160–2.
2. See e.g. Sydney Janet Kaplan, *Katherine Mansfield and the Origins of Modernist Fiction* (Ithaca, NY: Cornell University Press, 1991), ch. 9; Patricia Moran, *Word of Mouth: Body Language in Katherine Mansfield and Virginia Woolf* (Charlottesville, Va.: University Press of Virginia, 1996); Angela Smith, *Katherine Mansfield and Virginia Woolf: A Public of Two* (Oxford: Clarendon Press, 1999).
3. *The Diary of Virginia Woolf,* ed. Anne Olivier Bell, 5 vols. (London: Hogarth Press, 1977–84), i. 243: 'The truth is, I suppose, that one of the conditions unexpressed but understood of our friendship has been precisely that it was almost entirely founded on quicksands'. The diary entry concerns Woolf's 'queer balance of interest, amusement, & annoyance' with regard to Mansfield (i. 242–3).
4. Angela Smith, *Katherine Mansfield: A Literary Life* (Basingstoke: Palgrave, 2000), 115.
5. See *The Critical Writings of Katherine Mansfield*, ed. Clare Hanson (Basingstoke: Macmillan, 1987), 56–63, 52–4.
6. *The Letters of Virginia Woolf*, ed. Nigel Nicolson, 6 vols. (London: Hogarth Press, 1975–80), ii. 144.
7. Ibid. ii.159.
8. Woolf, *Diary*, i. 258.
9. Ibid. ii. 43–4.
10. Ibid. ii. 61.
11. Ibid. ii. 44.
12. Ibid. ii. 62, 61.
13. Woolf, *Letters*, iv. 366.
14. Woolf, *Diary*, ii. 226–7.
15. See Claire Tomalin's remark that Mansfield was 'a liar all her life' (*SL* 57).

16. Woolf uses the same word in at least one other diary entry: see Woolf, *Diary*, i. 257.

17. As Ian Gordon comments, Murry's edition of the *Journal* is 'a brilliant piece of literary synthesis and editorial patchwork' (*CR* 78).

CHAPTER 2. 'THIS SECRET DISRUPTION': KATHERINE MANSFIELD'S IDENTITIES

1. Quoted in Angela Smith, *Katherine Mansfield: A Literary Life* (Basingstoke: Palgrave, 2000), 40.

2. Sydney Janet Kaplan, *Katherine Mansfield and the Origins of Modernist Fiction* (Ithaca, NY: Cornell University Press, 1991), 169.

3. See *KMN* i. 104, 176, 177; *SL* 69, 88, 90; *CLKM*, i. 27, 108, 163, 198, 239, 271 and *passim*; *CLKM* ii. 136 and *passim*; *CLKM* iv. 157, 307 and *passim*; *L.* 96, 99, 119; Smith, *Literary Life*, 47.

4. Quoted in *L.* 83.

5. Smith, *Literary Life*, 47; see also Mary Burgan's comment that dress was, for Mansfield, 'always a form of costume which served the intricacies of role-playing' (*Illness, Gender and Writing: The Case of Katherine Mansfield* (Baltimore: Johns Hopkins University Press, 1994), 50).

6. W. H. New, *Reading Mansfield and Metaphors of Form* (Montreal: McGill-Queen's University Press, 1999), 177.

7. C. K. Stead, 'Katherine Mansfield and T. S. Eliot: A Double Centenary', in Stead, *Answering to the Language: Essays on Modern Writers* (Auckland: Auckland University Press, 1989), 160.

8. 'Eerily prescient' is Sydney Kaplan's phrase in *Origins of Modernist Fiction*, 53.

9. See T. S. Eliot, 'Tradition and the Individual Talent', in *Selected Prose*, ed. Frank Kermode (London: Faber & Faber, 1975), 37–44; see also Maud Ellmann, *The Poetics of Impersonality: T. S. Eliot and Ezra Pound* (Brighton: Harvester, 1987).

10. See Keats's letter to Benjamin Bailey of 22 November 1817 in *Letters of John Keats*, ed. Robert Gittings (Oxford: Oxford University Press, 1970), 36–9.

CHAPTER 3. 'HESITATIONS, DOUBTS, BEGINNINGS'

1. See also Elizabeth Bowen on Mansfield's 'tentative, responsive, exploratory' art (*CR* 71), and Sydney Janet Kaplan, *Katherine Mansfield and the Origins of Modernist Fiction* (Ithaca, NY: Cornell

University Press, 1991), 152, on Mansfield's 'indirection, implicit suggestion, shifts in tone, juxtaposition of incongruities'; and see Kaplan's comments on the 'gaps, silences, sexual encodings, pre-oedipal rhythms [and] the fluidity and multiplicity' of Mansfield's prose as related to notions of *écriture féminine* (p. 158).

2. See William Shakespeare, *Hamlet, Prince of Denmark*, ed. Philip Edwards (Cambridge: Cambridge University Press, 1985), III.i.79; for Mansfield's comment on New Zealand as an 'undiscovered country', see *KMN* ii. 32.

3. William Wordsworth, *The Prelude: The Four Texts* (1798, 1799, 1805, 1850), ed. Jonathan Wordsworth (London: Penguin, 1995), 241 (1850, book vi, line 593).

CHAPTER 4.   KATHERINE MANSFIELD'S 'VAGRANT SELF'

1. Roger Robinson, 'Introduction: In from the Margin', in Robinson (ed.), *In from the Margin* (Baton Rouge, La.: Louisiana State University Press, 1994), 4.

2. C. K. Stead, 'Katherine Mansfield and T. S. Eliot: A Double Centenary', in Stead, *Answering to the Language: Essays on Modern Writers* (Auckland: Auckland University Press, 1989), 160.

3. C. K. Stead, 'Katherine Mansfield's Life', in ibid. 166.

4. See *Katherine Mansfield: Selected Letters*, ed. Vincent O'Sullivan (Oxford: Oxford University Press, 1989), 257.

5. Quoted in Angela Smith, *Katherine Mansfield: A Literary Life* (Basingstoke: Palgrave, 2000), 1.

6. Stead, 'Life', 167.

7. C. K. Stead, 'Katherine Mansfield as Colonial Realist', in Stead, *The Writer at Work* (Dunedin: University of Otago Press, 2000), 38.

8. Angela Smith, *Katherine Mansfield and Virginia Woolf: A Public of Two* (Oxford: Clarendon Press, 1999), 119. See also Smith, *Literary Life*, 88–94; and see p. 13, on 'The Woman at the Store' as Mansfield's 'most overtly disorientating story'.

9. *The Critical Writings of Katherine Mansfield*, ed. Clare Hanson (Basingstoke: Macmillan, 1987), 102.

CHAPTER 5.   'A QUEER STATE': WRITING GENDER AND SEXUALITY

1. See Virginia Woolf's comment that for Mansfield 'the writing self was a queer self' (*CR* 16).

2. In part, at least, Mansfield is referring to a recurrent issue in her relationship with Murry, the fact that Murry expected her to fulfil the 'female' duties of housekeeper, considering his own writing, reviewing, and editing of more importance than her work: see e.g. *CLKM* i. 125–6.
3. Mary Burgan, *Illness, Gender and Writing: The Case of Katherine Mansfield* (Baltimore: Johns Hopkins University Press, 1994), 42.
4. Sydney Janet Kaplan, *Katherine Mansfield and the Origins of Modernist Fiction* (Ithaca, NY: Cornell University Press, 1991), 35. See also Kaplan's distinction between the way that Wilde's influence 'makes itself felt' in Mansfield's writing through 'experimentation and *impersonation*' while, by contrast, Chekhov's is 'bound up with a drive toward achievement and approval, maturity of *impersonality*' (p. 199).
5. Ibid. 11.
6. Kate Fullbrook, *Katherine Mansfield* (Brighton: Harvester, 1986).
7. See a letter from London of September 1908 where Mansfield records attending a suffragette meeting but leaving feeling that 'I could not be a suffragette – the world [is] too full of laughter' (*CLKM* i. 60); and Clare Hanson quotes an early sketch of what she calls 'quite awesome sentimentality' where Mansfield imagines taking feminists home where she would 'show them my babies [. . .] and put them in teagowns and then cuddle them – I think they would never go back to their Physical Culture, or the Society for the Promotion of Women's Rights' (*The Critical Writings of Katherine Mansfield* (Basingstoke: Macmillan, 1987), 19).
8. Kaplan, *Origins of Modernist Fiction*, 135; compare Angela Smith's comments on Mansfield's analysis of 'the ways in which women restrict themselves by acquiescing in the dictation of patriarchy' (*Katherine Mansfield: A Literary Life* (Basingstoke: Palgrave, 2000), 40).
9. Another reference to the suffragette movement in Mansfield's work may be encoded within 'The Doves' Nest'. Pamela Dunbar suggests that the name of Millie Fawcett involves an allusion to the 'well-known writer and campaigner for women's suffrage', Dame Millicent Fawcett, and argues that 'the implication here is of course a feminist one', since her name implies that Millie will eventually get 'her revenge on her forceful future husband', Mr Prodger, by 'becoming a pioneer of women's rights' (Dunbar, *Radical Mansfield: Double Discourse in Katherine Mansfield's Short Stories* (Basingstoke: Macmillan, 1997) 122). An alternative reading, however, would see the allusion as an ironic commentary on Millie's *lack* of feminism, her 'feminine' acquiescence in a story that is highly concerned with – and troubled by – women's complicity with patriarchy.
10. Kaplan, *Origins of Modernist Fiction*, 44–5.

11. Ruth Parkin-Gounelas, 'Katherine Mansfield Reading Other Women: The Personality of the Text', in Roger Robinson (ed.), *Katherine Mansfield: In from the Margin* (Baton Rouge, La.: Louisiana State University Press, 1994), 47.
12. See Joan Riviere, 'Womanliness as Masquerade', in Victor Burgin *et al.* (eds.), *Formations of Fantasy* (London: Methuen, 1986), 35–44.
13. For a recent, influential discussion of the 'performance' of gender, see Judith Butler, *Gender Trouble: Feminism and the Subversion of Identity* (New York: Routledge, 1990).
14. Dunbar, *Radical Mansfield*, 81
15. *The Letters of Virginia Woolf*, ed. Nigel Nicolson, 6 vols. (London: Hogarth Press, 1975–80), iv. 366.
16. Dunbar, *Radical Mansfield*, p. ix.

CHAPTER 6.   'THE GRASS WAS BLUE': 'PRELUDE' AND 'AT THE BAY'

1. Sydney Kaplan uses the first part of this sentence as an epigraph in *Katherine Mansfield and the Origins of Modernist Fiction* (Ithaca, NY: Cornell University Press, 1991), 103. Pater's book was an important influence on Mansfield: see Angela Smith's comment that the 'Conclusion' to *The Renaissance* was a 'pivotal text' for Mansfield in *Katherine Mansfield: A Literary Life* (Basingstoke: Palgrave, 2000), 33.
2. Compare Elizabeth Bowen's comments on the stories as 'growing' 'not only from memory but from longing' ('Introduction' to *34 Short Stories* (London: Collins, 1957), 25).
3. There are in fact twenty-one stories included in the 'Burnell' section of *Undiscovered Country: The New Zealand Stories of Katherine Mansfield*, ed. Ian A. Gordon (London: Longman, 1974).
4. See Sydney Janet Kaplan, *Origins of Modernist Fiction*, 216; the phrase 'serial novel' is from a letter to Charlotte Perkins of March 1922, quoted by Gillian Boddy, ' "Finding the Treasure", Coming Home: Katherine Mansfield in 1921–1922', in Roger Robinson (ed.), *Katherine Mansfield: In from the Margin* (Baton Rouge, La.: Louisiana State University Press, 1994), 186.
5. Quoted in Katherine Mansfield, *The Aloe, with Prelude*, ed. Vincent O'Sullivan (Manchester: Carcanet New Press, 1983), 164.
6. Mrs Fairfield, whose name is a translation of the French Beauchamp, is, in fact, based not on a Beauchamp at all, but on Mansfield's maternal grandmother, whose name was Margaret Mansfield Dyer. One might speculate on the way that the name of the grandmother in the two stories both disguises and, at the same

time, highlights the coded presence of death in the name of Mrs
Fairfield's original, Mrs Dyer.
7. 'At the Bay' was written between the end of July and 10 September
1921: see *L.* 339; *SKM* 571.

CHAPTER 7.   THE 'OTHER PASSION'

1. Quoted in *L.*, 234.
2. Elizabeth Bowen, 'Introduction' to *34 Short Stories* (London: Collins,
1957), 18.
3. Brophy's extraordinary essay 'Katherine Mansfield's Self-Depic-
tion', originally published in 1966, links Mansfield's 'aggression'
with her mother's lack of affection for her, arguing that her
mother's withdrawal of milk is linked to Mansfield's multiple
identifications, her aggression, her tuberculosis, an alleged (and
probably fictional) abortion, and her 'cannibalistic imagination'.
Brophy's most outrageous claim, perhaps, is that Mansfield's
tuberculosis was 'psychosomatic', that at the age of 31 Mansfield
was 'ill with anger', and that knowing that her mother 'would have
preferred not to [have given] her birth' led to a kind of suicide: 'she
arranged, as it were, for her mother to have a postdated abortion –
of herself' (*CR* 89–94). Despite these wild and often ill-founded
conjectures and allegations (generated no doubt by her attempt to
challenge Murry's representation of Mansfield as too 'sensitive' for
life – 'if anything, she was too brutal for life', Brophy comments),
Brophy's essay is useful in highlighting the topic of the present
chapter, the significance of aggression in Mansfield's writing. See
also Vincent O'Sullivan's comments on the 'possibility of savagery'
in Mansfield (*CR* 145–6); and see Pamela Dunbar, *Radical Mansfield:
Double Discourse in Katherine Mansfield's Short Stories* (Basingstoke:
Macmillan, 1997), for a reading of the stories as veiled critiques of –
veiled aggression towards – her society.
4. Later in life, Mansfield thought of *In a German Pension* as 'a lie', and
considered it 'positively *juvenile*' and '*immature*': '*its just not good
enough*', she comments (*CLKM* iii. 206).
5. Compare Raymond Mortimer's comments in another early review
that Mansfield never 'portrayed a really agreeable person' (*CR* 13).
6. *The Diary of Virginia Woolf*, ed. Anne Olivier Bell, 5 vols. (London:
Hogarth Press, 1977–84), i. 216. The reference is to 'the long story
she has written', but, since the entry is dated 9 November 1918, we
can infer that Woolf is referring to 'Je ne parle pas français' (see *SL*
180).

7. Mary Burgan, *Illness, Gender and Writing: The Case of Katherine Mansfield* (Baltimore: Johns Hopkins University Press, 1994), 47.
8. It is significant that Duquette is just about to publish what he calls his 'serial story', *Wrong Doors*, and that Mansfield referred to her prospective New Zealand novel as a 'serial novel' in a letter of March 1921 (quoted in Gillian Boddy, '"Finding the Treasure", Coming Home: Katherine Mansfield in 1921–1922', in Roger Robinson (ed.), *Katherine Mansfield: In from the Margin* (Baton Rouge, La.: Louisiana State University Press, 1994), 186).
9. Sydney Janet Kaplan, *Katherine Mansfield and the Origins of Modernist Fiction* (Ithaca, NY: Cornell University Press, 1991), 183.
10. Ibid. 187.
11. 'Je ne parle pas français' was originally published in a small press edition in 1920. When it was included in the Constable edition of *Bliss and Other Stories*, the editor, Michael Sadleir, demanded a number of cuts to make it more palatable and to blur the edges of its vicious satire on Duquette's sexuality: the reference to virgins was cut, as was a reference to the full extent of the African laundress's abuse of the 10-year-old Duquette (she used to 'open her bodice and put me to her', he says (*SS* 147)), together with the story's original ending, where Duquette contemplates sleeping with the café's 'madame'.
12. Disgust is included in the final sentences of the full, unexpurgated version as Duquette imagines the moles on the skin of the café-owner: 'They remind me somehow, disgustingly, of mushrooms' (*SS* 167); Duquette also comments on 'things about my submerged life that really were disgusting and never could possibly see the light of literary day' (*SS* 151).

CHAPTER 8.   CONCLUSION: INTERRUPTION

1. Compare Elizabeth Bowen's comment on a theme that was almost an obsession for Mansfield, the 'wrecking of an illusion' ('Introduction', to *34 Short Stories* (London: Collins, 1957), 17).
2. Mansfield often declared her intention to write a novel, in fact: see, for example, *CLKM* iv. 273, where she tells her agent J. B. Pinker that 'I mean to write a novel. I long to'. And her awareness, her self-consciousness, about the length of her own fictions is apparent from her reviews of others' novels where she often refers to their length and to the question of whether they earn their length. 'Is this, we wonder, turning over its three hundred and sixty-eight pages, to be the novel of the future?', she asks of one novel. Jane Mander's *The Story of a New Zealand River* is even longer at 'four hundred and

thirty-two pages of small type': 'why is her book not half as long, twice as honest?', Mansfield asks. And Hugh Walpole's *The Captives* weighs in at a dismaying 'four hundred and seventy pages, packed as tight as they can be with an assortment of strange creatures and furnishings' (*The Critical Writings of Katherine Mansfield*, ed. Clare Hanson (Basingstoke: Macmillan, 1987), 90, 102, 105).

Select Bibliography

WORKS BY KATHERINE MANSFIELD

Separate Story Collections

In a German Pension (London: Stephen Swift, 1911).
Bliss and Other Stories (London: Constable, 1920).
The Garden Party and Other Stories (London: Constable, 1922).
The Doves' Nest and Other Stories, ed. John Middleton Murry (London: Constable, 1923).
Something Childish and Other Stories, ed. John Middleton Murry (London: Constable, 1924); and in the USA as *The Little Girl and Other Stories* (New York: Knopf, 1924).

Stories Published Separately

Prelude (Richmond: Hogarth Press, 1918).
Je ne parle pas français (Hampstead: Heron Press, 1920).
The Aloe, ed. John Middleton Murry (London: Constable, 1930).
The Aloe, with Prelude, ed. Vincent O'Sullivan (Manchester: Carcanet New Press, 1983).

Collected and Selected Editions of the Short Stories

Collected Stories of Katherine Mansfield (London: Constable, 1945); republished in paperback (London: Penguin, 1981).
34 Short Stories, ed. Elizabeth Bowen (London: Collins, 1957).
Selected Stories, ed. D. M. Dent (Oxford: Oxford University Press, 1981).
Short Stories, ed. Claire Tomalin (London: Dent, 1983).
The Stories of Katherine Mansfield, ed. Antony Alpers (Auckland: Oxford University Press, 1984).
Selected Stories, ed. Angela Smith (Oxford University Press, 2002).

Other Works

Poems, ed. John Middleton Murry (London: Constable, 1923).

The Journal of Katherine Mansfield, ed. John Middleton Murry (London: Constable, 1927).

The Letters of Katherine Mansfield, ed. John Middleton Murry, 2 vols. (London: Constable, 1928). Now superseded by O'Sullivan and Scott's Clarendon Press edition, except for the letters from 1922 in the second volume.

Novels and Novelists, ed. John Middleton Murry (London: Constable, 1930). A selection of Mansfield's reviews.

The Scrapbook of Katherine Mansfield, ed. John Middleton Murry (London: Constable, 1937).

Katherine Mansfield's Letters to John Middleton Murry, 1913–1922, ed. John Middleton Murry (London: Constable, 1951).

Journal of Katherine Mansfield: The Definitive Edition, ed. John Middleton Murry (London: Constable, 1954). Not in fact 'definitive' and now superseded by Margaret Scott's edition.

Undiscovered Country: The New Zealand Stories of Katherine Mansfield, ed. Ian A. Gordon (London: Longman, 1974).

The Letters and Journals of Katherine Mansfield: A Selection, ed. C. K. Stead (London: Allen Lane, 1977).

The Urewera Notebook, ed. Ian A. Gordon (Oxford: Oxford University Press, 1978).

The Collected Letters of Katherine Mansfield, ed. Vincent O'Sullivan and Margaret Scott, 4 vols. to date (Oxford: Clarendon Press, 1984–96). The definitive edition of the letters, which needs to be supplemented, until the publication of vol. v, by Murry's edition of the letters, vol. ii.

The Critical Writings of Katherine Mansfield, ed. Clare Hanson (Basingstoke: Macmillan, 1987).

Poems of Katherine Mansfield, ed. Vincent O'Sullivan (Auckland: Oxford University Press, 1988).

Katherine Mansfield: Selected Letters, ed. Vincent O'Sullivan (Oxford: Oxford University Press, 1989).

The Katherine Mansfield Notebooks, ed. Margaret Scott, 2 vols. (Canterbury, NZ: Lincoln University Press 1997). An accurate scholarly edition of the notebooks.

Bibliography

Kirkpatrick, B. J., *A Bibliography of Katherine Mansfield* (Oxford: Clarendon Press, 1989). The most complete bibliography of Mansfield's work and secondary materials.

Williams, Mark, 'Katherine Mansfield', in *Post-Colonial Literatures in English: Southeast Asian, New Zealand, and the Pacific, 1970–1992* (New York: G. K. Hall, 1990). An annotated bibliography of criticism on Mansfield.

Biography

Alpers, Antony, *The Life of Katherine Mansfield* (London; Jonathan Cape, 1980). The fullest, and generally acknowledged to be the standard biography.

Meyers, Jeffrey, *Katherine Mansfield: A Biography* (New York: New Directions, 1978).

Smith, Angela, *Katherine Mansfield: A Literary Life* (Basingstoke: Palgrave, 2000). A useful short life focusing in particular on Mansfield's New Zealand origins and on the influence of post-Impressionism and Fauvism on her work.

Tomalin, Claire, *Katherine Mansfield: A Secret Life* (1987; London: Penguin, 1988). Builds on Alpers's and others' biographies but with important revisions particularly with regard to questions of health, gender, and sexuality.

CRITICISM

Boddy, Gillian, *Katherine Mansfield: The Woman and the Writer* (Harmondsworth: Penguin, 1988).

Burgan, Mary, *Illness, Gender and Writing: The Case of Katherine Mansfield* (Baltimore: Johns Hopkins University Press, 1994). A psychoanalytically informed study of the representation of the body in Mansfield's work, focusing on issues of illness, body-image, food, homosexuality, reproduction, sexuality, and hysteria in Mansfield's life and writing.

Dunbar, Pamela, *Radical Mansfield: Double Discourse in Katherine Mansfield's Short Stories* (Basingstoke: Macmillan, 1997). Argues that Mansfield's work involves a radical critique of social institutions and personal relationships – including gender roles, the family, and sexuality – largely veiled by an 'impeccable surface lyricism'.

Fullbrook, Kate, *Katherine Mansfield* (Brighton: Harvester, 1986). An influential feminist study of Mansfield's work.

Hankin, C. A., *Katherine Mansfield and her Confessional Stories* (London: Macmillan, 1983).

Hanson, Clare, *Short Stories and Short Fictions, 1880–1980* (London: Macmillan, 1985). Includes a chapter on Mansfield's stories.

—— and Gurr, Andrew, *Katherine Mansfield* (London: Macmillan,

1981). A useful short introductory study.

Kaplan, Sydney Janet, *Katherine Mansfield and the Origins of Modernist Fiction* (Ithaca, NY: Cornell University Press, 1991). An important study that puts Mansfield at the centre of the modernist project, with useful chapters on the influence of Wilde, Woolf, sexuality, the city, genre, modernism, feminism, and impersonation.

Kobler, J. F., *Katherine Mansfield: A Study in the Short Fiction* (Boston: Twayne, 1990).

Moran, Patricia, *Word of Mouth: Body Language in Katherine Mansfield and Virginia Woolf* (Charlottesville, Va.: University Press of Virginia, 1996). A feminist reading of the two writers, focusing on issues of the body, hysteria, food, and mothering.

Nathan, R. B., *Katherine Mansfield* (New York: Continuum, 1988).

—— (ed.), *Critical Essays on Katherine Mansfield* (New York: G. K. Hall., 1993). Includes a wide range of critical essays, reprinted and new, grouped into three sections: the colonialist contexts of her writing, biography, and formalist studies.

New, W. H., *Reading Mansfield and Metaphors of Form* (Montreal: McGill-Queen's University Press, 1999). A wide-ranging study concerned with Mansfield as a 'colonial' writer but concentrating on formalist analysis of the stories.

Paulette Michel and Dupuis, Michel (eds.), *The Fine Instrument: Essays on Katherine Mansfield* (Aarhus: Dangaroo Press, 1989).

Pilditch, Jan (ed.), *The Critical Response to Katherine Mansfield* (Westport, Conn.: Greenwood, 1996). A useful collection of essays, ranging from the first reviews to essays published to mark the centenary of Mansfield's birth. Includes influential contributions by V. S. Pritchett, David Daiches, Elizabeth Bowen, Ian A. Gordon, Margaret Scott, Vincent O'Sullivan, C. K. Stead, and others.

Robinson, Roger (ed.), *Katherine Mansfield: In from the Margin* (Baton Rouge, La.: Louisiana State University Press, 1994). An important collection of essays from two centennial conferences held in 1988.

Smith, Angela, *Katherine Mansfield and Virginia Woolf: A Public of Two* (Oxford: Clarendon Press, 1999). An impressive revaluation of the relationship of the two writers, with a Kristevan analysis of abjection and liminality in Mansfield's work.

Index

see also notebooks
Karori, 58
letters, 1, 5, 8, 10, 12, 13, 19–21, 22, 23, 27, 32, 34, 37, 44, 45, 57, 59-60, 63, 69–72, 73–4, 84, 87, 89
'Life of Ma Parker', 33
'The Little Girl', 49, 58
'The Little Governess', 33, 53–4, 73
'The Man without a Temperament', 27, 33, 73
'A Married Man's Story', 52, 55–6, 73, 81
'Marriage à la Mode', 33, 52
'Millie', 36–7, 38, 39–40, 41–3
'Miss Brill', 20, 23, 54
'Mr and Mrs Dove', 27, 52
'Mr Reginald Peacock's Day', 52, 73
notebooks, 1, 5, 8, 12, 13–19, 34–6, 44, 45–7, 69–70, 81, 84
Novels and Novelists, 4
'Ole Underwood', 36–8, 39, 40
'Pictures', 33, 53
poems, 4
Prelude, 4, 5, 33, 36, 49, 50–1, 52, 55, 57–63, 64, 68, 70, 73, 80
'Psychology', 27, 28–31
reviews, 4, 5
The Scrapbook of Katherine Mansfield, 5
'Silhouettes', 2
'The Singing Lesson', 54
'The Stranger', 27, 33, 52
'Vignette', 2

'The Voyage', 26–7, 31, 33
'The Woman at the Store', 3, 33, 36–9, 40–1, 52
'The Young Girl', 52, 73
Mahupuka, Maata, 14
marriage, 2, 3, 11
modernism, 20, 29
Moran, Patricia, 83
Morrell, Ottoline, 27, 69
Mortimer, Raymond, 17–18, 88
Murry, John Middleton, 3, 4, 7, 8–9, 10, 12, 32, 35, 36, 37, 44–5, 47, 57, 69, 70, 73, 74, 86, 88

names, 11
Native Companion, 2
New Age, 2
New Zealand, 1–2, 4, 13–14, 23, 32, 33, 34–43, 46–7, 57, 58, 63, 85
nomadism, 3, 32–4, 36, 37, 43

Orage, A. R., 2
O'Sullivan, Vincent, 8, 23, 79

Parkin-Gounelas, Ruth, 50
Pater, Walter, 14
  Child in the House, 13
  The Renaissance, 57, 87
Payne, Sylvia, 33
Perkins, Charlotte, 87
personal identity, multiple, 8, 9, 10–21, 32, 36, 43, 81
postmodernism, 29
Pound, Ezra, 72
psychoanalysis, 14–15, 16, 29

Queen's College, 2, 34
Queen Victoria, 42